THE
INGREDIENTS
FOR GREAT
TEACHING

Sara Miller McCune founded SAGE Publishing in 1965 to support the dissemination of usable knowledge and educate a global community. SAGE publishes more than 1000 journals and over 800 new books each year, spanning a wide range of subject areas. Our growing selection of library products includes archives, data, case studies and video. SAGE remains majority owned by our founder and after her lifetime will become owned by a charitable trust that secures the company's continued independence.

Los Angeles | London | New Delhi | Singapore | Washington DC | Melbourne

FOREWORD BY
DANIEL T. WILLINGHAM

THE
INGREDIENTS
FOR GREAT
TEACHING

PEDRO DE BRUYCKERE

Los Angeles | London | New Delhi
Singapore | Washington DC | Melbourne

Los Angeles | London | New Delhi
Singapore | Washington DC | Melbourne

SAGE Publications Ltd
1 Oliver's Yard
55 City Road
London EC1Y 1SP

SAGE Publications Inc.
2455 Teller Road
Thousand Oaks, California 91320

SAGE Publications India Pvt Ltd
B 1/I 1 Mohan Cooperative Industrial Area
Mathura Road
New Delhi 110 044

SAGE Publications Asia-Pacific Pte Ltd
3 Church Street
#10-04 Samsung Hub
Singapore 049483

Editor: James Clark
Assistant editor: Robert Patterson
Production editor: Nicola Carrier
Copyeditor: Jill Birch
Indexer: Gary Kirby
Marketing manager: Dilhara Attygalle
Cover design: Sheila Tong
Typeset by: C&M Digitals (P) Ltd, Chennai, India
Printed in the UK

Library of Congress Control Number: 2017951429

British Library Cataloguing in Publication data

A catalogue record for this book is available from the British Library

ISBN 978-1-52642-338-2
ISBN 978-1-52642-339-9 (pbk)

At SAGE we take sustainability seriously. Most of our products are printed in the UK using responsibly sourced papers and boards. When we print overseas we ensure sustainable papers are used as measured by the PREPS grading system. We undertake an annual audit to monitor our sustainability.

CONTENTS

LIST OF FIGURES AND TABLES

Figures

Tables

ABOUT THE AUTHOR

 Pedro De Bruyckere (PhD) is an educational scientist at Arteveldehogeschool in Ghent, Belgium, were he has trained future teachers since 2001. Before studying pedagogy, Pedro was a teacher himself, teaching Dutch, history and geography. He has co-written several books on youth and education in Dutch and is often asked to be an international public speaker on education.

In 2015 Pedro co-wrote the popular book *Urban myths about learning and education* with Paul Kirschner and Casper Hulshof. He is also an avid blogger on new research in education; do check out his blog: www.theeconomyofmeaning.com.

One of his strongest points is that he is funny in explaining serious stuff. And now for something completely different: you can always ask Pedro something about guitars, but do be warned, he will talk even more about six strings than he does about education. He does wonder who will have read this to the end.

ACKNOWLEDGEMENTS

Acknowledgements always remind me of the Oscars, long before they started to play music to signal that the famous actress or director had to leave the stage. There are so many people you need to thank, but at the same time you know for sure you will forget people. For those I will forget to mention, I'm sorry. You are always on my mind, just not at the time I had to finish this. Do remind me of this and I'll buy you a Coke.

During the past nine years I have been lucky enough to co-write several books with great minds. Bert Smits, Linda Duits and, of course, Paul Kirschner and Casper Hulshof. Without them I wouldn't have become the educational writer I am today. Also for the publishers who have taken the risk to publish something I've written on trains, planes and indoor play centres – don't ask – a big thank you. And James, I will never forget that you stalked me even in Sweden to sign with you, thank you!

There are also many people who have inspired or triggered me in past years. Besides my students and colleagues at Arteveldehogeschool University College, there is Bengt Sonderhall, Tom Bennett, Niels and Jan Tishauer, Erik Kalenze and all the other fine people I've met via researchED such as Dylan, Dan, David, Carl, Yana, Lucy, Sara, Eva, Christian, Ian, Glenn and the infamous many, many others.

But there is one group I need to thank the most: they are the teachers who brought me here. They helped me to beat the statistics. It's because of them I try to play my part in making education better, because they showed me education and great teachers do make the difference. They did for me; I hope I can help people to do the same. Yes, I had some teachers who delivered great examples for my students how not to act, but the majority of them were inspiring, challenging and at the same time just normal people like you and me.

The final words are for Helena and our boys. No words to describe what you all mean to me, but boys, when you finally have learned to read English, you'll see I write the same lame jokes in every language.

FOREWORD

Many of today's teachers are suspicious of the usefulness of science to their profession, and it's easy to see why. Sometimes they are told to do things that their experience tells them will not work or that seem plain crazy. Furthermore, the science of education has always held first place in the contest for most fickle practitioners, beating out even nutritionists; what educationalists describe as schooling's 'health food' will be 'junk food' next year. And at its worst, claims that research supports one practice or another are all too often made without any research backing at all. Such claims are nothing but a cudgel to get a teacher to do what an administrator or lawmaker has dreamed up.

The truth is that drawing on science to improve educational practice is fraught with challenges. The first challenge concerns relevance. What a scientist observes about children's learning may be consistent in the laboratory, but many not apply in the classroom. Or it may apply in a classroom composed of middle-class 14-year-olds with a male teacher, but not a classroom of disadvantaged 9-year-olds with a female teacher.

Even if we're sure that our scientific findings are broadly relevant to classrooms, there's a second challenge. Those pitching the wares of scientists must think about how the interventions they advocate fit into a teacher's broader practice. For example, much has been made in the last few years about spaced practice—having some time pass between work sessions. It's easy to advocate for this technique, but implementing it might be quite disruptive. What is the new, spaced practice session displacing? In some cases—for example, differentiated instruction—people demand nothing less than a significant overhaul to teaching practice, in order to put in place practices that researchers claim will help kids. Then too, teachers seldom have complete freedom to change their practice. They are constrained by school-wide policy or by laws constraining the shape of the school day or the curriculum.

Scientists have mostly neglected thinking about how research findings actually fit into a teacher's day, but they can almost be forgiven for this oversight. They simply don't know much about classrooms. But the final challenge in applying science to education concerns a matter that scientists *do* know about, yet have seldom articulated to educators in any detail—the probabilistic nature of scientific conclusions. When scientists learn something of potential utility in the teaching of reading, for example, or about how children understand mathematics, that knowledge can be reliable without being universal. It may apply to most children under most circumstances (but not all under all) yet still be scientific and still be worth knowing.

So, with these three grand challenges before us—application, relevance, and communication—should teachers bother with science? What are the chances that a scientist will get it right?

Pedro De Bruyckere's writing is worth every teacher's time. Pedro has been deeply immersed in the very issues I've described here, thinking through not just the science behind pedagogical strategies, but how they might fit in a teacher's practice and how best to communicate to educators why he thinks they should consider engaging that practice. Pedro is so persuaded of the importance of these issues he has risked some of his personal fortune to publicize them. He approached a Dutch publisher with the idea of distributing a translation of a book I had written on this topic, and when the publisher expressed doubt that the book would sell, Pedro wagered dinner at a Michelin-starred restaurant that the book would at least break even (to my knowledge the winner of this bet is, as yet, undetermined).

More important than Pedro's dedication to getting the science of education right is the product of that dedication. The book you hold in your hands is a *tour de force*. The backbone is the author's sophistication in research methodology that enables him to snuff out fake science. At least as important, however, is Pedro's extraordinary breadth of scholarship; his knowledge of children's minds and hearts allows him to anticipate far-ranging consequences of prospective classroom interventions and to see probable costs and benefits beyond the strict limits of a research protocol. At the same time, everything you'll read here is filtered through common sense about classroom realities.

Enjoy and profit from this book. I know I will turn to it again and again for deeper understanding about how to help children learn.

Daniel T. Willingham
Professor
Department of Psychology
University of Virginia

1

COOKING, MEDICINE AND EVIDENCE

This chapter will explore the following questions:

- Why is it impossible to have clear recipes in education?
- What do average effect sizes in educational research hide?
- What is the difference between evidence-based and evidence-informed education?

The moral of the burnt steak...

What is the secret of a masterchef? Of course, he or she probably has access to the very best ingredients, but even a simple egg fried by a star-rated chef is better than what an average family gets on their breakfast plates each morning. On the other hand, using the best ingredients is not, by itself, a guarantee of success. Here I am speaking from bitter personal experience, since I once rendered a delicious (and very expensive) piece of Wagyu steak wholly inedible!

Too much salt, not enough pepper, too sour, too sweet: all of these things are possible, in addition to too raw and (in my case) too burnt. The difference between a masterchef and a master bungler is the difference in the extent to which a person possesses the necessary techniques that allow them to make best possible use of the ingredients at their disposal.

It is exactly the same in education. John Hattie[1] has repeatedly told us that almost everything in education has a positive effect, but that some things are more positive than others. The truth, however, is more complex than that. For example, reference is often made to the positive effect of feedback. But this does not mean that all forms of feedback result in better learning. Worse still, some types of feedback can actually have a negative impact. In much the same way, direct instruction and self-discovery learning have both acquired negative connotations in recent years, albeit from different groups in different places, and it has to be admitted that both are open to question. But should they both be consigned to the dustbin of educational history? No, that is not a good idea. Naturally, we also need to remember that some things, such as learning styles, have very little or no effect, but I have already written a book about that.[2]

Why masterchefs have it easier than teachers

In one sense, Gordon Ramsey, Heston Blumenthal and all the other world-famous chefs have it much easier than teachers. They have the luxury of just choosing a single recipe to make a perfect dish. Even then, things can sometimes go wrong, but don't underestimate the importance of having a single step-by-step plan. In most cases, it works, and works well. In this context, the difference between education and cooking is huge. No matter how much teachers (and policy-makers) would like it to be true, in education there is no such thing as a recipe that works in all circumstances. Policy mandarins might continue to dream of applying the Finnish recipe to our educational system, but a simple copy-and-paste of Finnish methods offers no guarantee that those methods will work with equal success when superimposed on a different country or region. This is frustrating, yet also a cause for optimism.

FURTHER THINKING: WHY THE EDUCATION PYRAMID CANNOT BE RIGHT

In our earlier book about educational myths, we talked about the Loch Ness monster of educational theory: the learning pyramid (see Figure 1.1). I do not intend to repeat the whole story here. But because it is relevant to what follows here, I would at least wish to re-emphasize the following conclusion: if the pyramid is right, then there really is a single method of teaching that works best in every context, for every purpose and with every pupil. But is that what we actually believe?

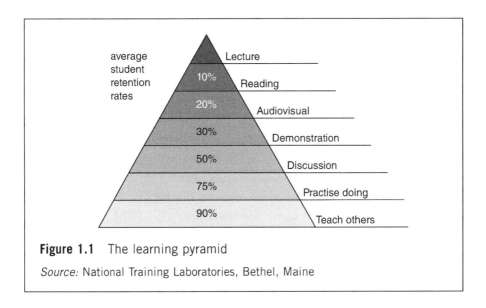

Figure 1.1   The learning pyramid

Source: National Training Laboratories, Bethel, Maine

Frustration

The lack of a one-stop recipe in education is frustrating because it means that there are seldom simple solutions to important educational challenges. When we were writing our book *Urban myths about learning and education*, we soon discovered that this desire for simple solutions was frequently an important part of the appeal of such myths. They offer, or seem to offer, quick and easy answers. In his book *When can you trust the experts?*, Daniel Willingham[3] warns us that these solutions are often mistakenly applied to different problems at the same time: do this, the theory says, because it works for dyslexia, ADHD, truancy and even sweaty feet! Okay, I admit that even teachers wouldn't try it on the last one. But there are some who would try it on just about everything else. What's more, simple solutions become even more attractive when teachers are under pressure. And in many cases, the teacher's job already involves above-average levels of stress. Educational policy-makers are also charmed by simple solutions, to some extent because they are uncertain about the quality (and qualities) of their own teaching staff. More than once in recent years we have seen the introduction of methods and materials that are supposedly 'teacher-proof'. In other words, methods and materials that even the biggest idiot in the world could use to obtain excellent results with any child.

(Of course, I exaggerate; but not by much.) Nowadays, there are even plans to introduce bots and robots in the classroom. By this, I don't mean the jazzy multi-coloured machines that help motivate pupils to develop their programming skills, but rather a series of smart applications that are intended to guide pupils through their learning process. This is no longer science fiction but science fact, and it is a dream that appeals to many. As long ago as 2011, Watson, the supercomputer developed by IBM, was able to beat the strongest candidate on the American TV quiz show *Jeopardy*. Since then, Watson has already been used to support doctors in their work[4] and the idea is to now do the same for teachers.[5] But IBM and Pearson, who are currently trying to sell Watson to the educational world, use a crucial word in their promotional blurb: support. Fortunately, the discussion is not about (or at least is no longer about) replacing teachers in the classroom, because even in our high-tech age of supercomputers and mega-apps people have finally come to realize that human interaction will always be a crucial part of the educational process.

FURTHER THINKING: JILL WATSON

Like most teachers, the number of emails I get from my students is in inverse proportion to the amount of time that remains before they need to hand in their next paper or before their next exams. Email is a fantastic invention, but one that seems to be costing us more and more of that precious commodity: time.

Imagine for a moment that you could use a robot to answer some of these mails. Many of the answers involve a standard text, because students tend to forget the same things or are too lazy to look them up. Often, it's just quicker and easier (for them) to ask the teacher. Professor Ashok Goel of the Georgia Institute of Technology suspects that in the near future it will be possible for everyone to answer 40% of such emails in this way. In fact, he knows it for certain, because he has already used this kind of smart technology with success. In recent months, his students have regularly received replies from his assistant, Miss Jill Watson, who answers their questions in a firm but friendly manner or else forwards the query on to the professor, if she does not know the answer herself. The students only very recently learnt that Miss Watson does not exist; or rather that she is not a real flesh-and-blood person.[6]

A cause for optimism

The very complexity of education is actually a cause for optimism, and this is for various reasons. Firstly, it makes clear that education is not something you can just 'do', almost without thinking. You see this sometimes in television programmes. A famous celebrity is dropped into a classroom and expected to play the role of 'teacher for a day'. Most of them don't make a very good job of it. Why? Because it's not as easy as it looks. The more people understand that education and teaching are complex matters, the greater the likelihood that the image of teachers will improve. The second reason for encouragement, at least in my humble opinion, is the fact that the very absence of simple, all-embracing solutions means that there are many roads leading to Rome. If you look at the results of educational research, you will soon discover that there are a variety of different methods that 'work'.

Lots of things work, but...

Even so, we need to be realistic. Lots of things work, but not always, not for everyone, not for every purpose and not in every context. I hope that the following two examples will serve to highlight this complexity.

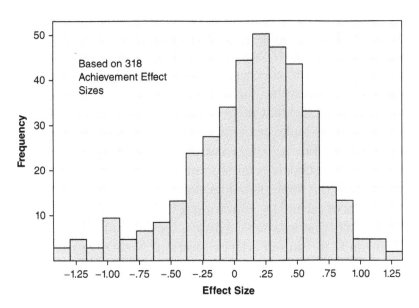

Figure 1.2   Electronic distance learning versus face-to-face instruction: Distribution of effect sizes (Clark and Mayer 2016, based on data from Bernard et al., 2004)

Take a look at the diagram on the previous page (Figure 1.2). It shows the effectiveness of particular courses of study and the extent to which those courses involved the use of online teaching methods.

In this graph you can see an overview of the 318 different effect sizes of studies measuring the different learning effect of electronic distance learning versus face-to-face instruction. With effect size scientists describe the magnitude of the result as it occurs. While in most statistics, there aren't any negative effect sizes, in discussions about learning negative effects are sometimes used to show that pupils have actually 'unlearned'. If you look at the graph if you want to know if digital learning is better or worse than face-to-face learning, the answer isn't clear-cut. The effectiveness results of the courses where the majority of the teaching was given online are to be found on both sides of the results spectrum. In other words, online courses belong in both the 'most effective' and 'least effective' categories. This means that it is easy to disprove the statement 'online teaching doesn't work' by simply looking at this graphic. It also shows, of course, that purpose, context and approach are all important in achieving success. This example is taken from the seminal work on technology in education by Clark and Mayer,[7] in which they take several hundred pages to explain what works, when, where and why (before adding a final 'maybe'...).

You can apply a similar reasoning to my second example: homework. In recent years, there have been an increasing number of pleas to abolish homework. If you consult John Hattie,[8] you will see that homework has a mean effect size of 0.29, which is not brilliant. Hattie only refers to 'added value' for scores of 0.40 and above.[9] However, it is important to realize that this score of 0.29 is a mean score, an average. If you start to make distinctions within the average, you soon see different results. Take age, for example. The learning effect of homework in primary schools is an abysmal 0.15, but this score increases dramatically as the pupils get older, so that by the time they reach the last two years of secondary education it has risen to a mean of 0.64.[10] Does this imply that we should give less (or no) homework in primary education and more in secondary education? No, it does not! The situation is much more complex than that. We first need to examine the content of the homework. What exactly does it involve? Homework that consists of simply completing a series of exercises will have much less effect than homework that serves as a basis for further development back in the classroom.[11] And the complexity doesn't stop there.

Where, for example, does the pupil do his or her homework? A child that has to do their homework in a noisy room packed with other members of the family will probably perform less well than a child that can work in a quiet room of their own. You can probably think of many more similar parameters without too much bother.

FURTHER THINKING: HOW CAN YOU BEST HELP YOUR CHILD WITH THEIR HOMEWORK?

A meta-study under the leadership of Maria Castro[12] examined the results of 37 research projects that investigated the influence of parents on the learning abilities of their children. The results were all published between 2000 and 2013 and covered age ranges running from nursery school to the end of compulsory education. These results revealed no fewer than 108 different elements through which parents can play an influencing role on the school performance of their offspring. The ranking of parental behaviour from greatest to least effect was as follows:

- The parents' own expectations (effect = 0.224)

- Talking with your children about school (effect = 0.200)

- Reading with your children (effect = 0.168)

- The way you bring up your children (effect = 0.130)

- Helping your children with their homework (effect = 0.024)

- Taking part as parents in school activities (effect = 0.010)

Some of these effects should come as no surprise; for example, the added value of reading with your children has been known for some time. However, the more limited effect of helping children with their homework may perhaps serve as new ammunition for the homework debate. The meta-study also looked at the school subjects most and least likely to be affected by parental behaviour. It seems that the positive effect is strongest for the arts, followed by the mother language, although this effect quickly declines for other subjects, such as reading, foreign languages, mathematics, and so on. As far as the sciences are concerned, parental behaviour can even have a negative effect (although this conclusion is based on only two of the 37 studies).

It is perhaps equally important to realize that receiving feedback from teachers is also very important for the learning development of the child. But if the parents' input to homework is too great, to whom is the teacher really giving feedback?

Consequently, the question we should be asking is not 'what works and what doesn't work?', but rather 'where and when does something work?' and to answer the latter question effectively, we also need to know how and why something works. This is the question we will seek to examine in this book. What's more, it is a question that educationalists need to keep continually at the back of their mind given the current trend towards more evidence-based education (EBE).

Evidence-based versus evidence-informed

Imagine you fall sick. Of course, I hope this doesn't happen, but if you do there is a good chance that you will need to take medication. Evidence-based medicine is an important source of inspiration for evidence-based education. This latter concept is a mouth-watering prospect for many educationalists: after all, an approved medicine can only be brought onto the market once it has been extensively tested in accordance with clear and strictly agreed protocols. Wouldn't it be wonderful if we could apply the same principles to education! Would it? I'm not so sure. The problem is that we would need to scrap all kinds of things within the existing educational system, not because a particular approach does not work, but simply because we are not certain of the extent to which that approach works. But there is more: evidence-based theory has a strong preference for randomized controlled trials. In these trials, a test population is randomly divided into two or more groups, usually one or more test groups and a single control group, to see if a particular approach has an added value. The random selection of the groups is designed to ensure that background elements will not influence the overall results. Unfortunately, this is not only an expensive methodology, but, more importantly, it is also not the best way to examine every type of educational approach. Gravemeijer and Kirschner[13] have commented correctly that there are certainly examples of situations where randomized controlled trials seemed to work well, but that it is nevertheless difficult to make the same stringent demands for education as are made for medicine. In 1987, Slavin postulated in more concrete terms a list of the requirements necessary for education to run parallel with medicine:

1. a control group (who are often given a placebo) in which neither the experts (doctors/educationalists) nor the researchers are aware of which test subjects are in which condition (double-blind);
2. random distribution of the participants over the different conditions (randomization);
3. comparability between the groups;
4. very large groups;
5. the need for statistically significant results.

Gravemeijer and Kirschner posed the following questions about these requirements:

> Can we really give the pupils in a control group a form of education (a placebo) that we know will have no effect or even a negative effect? And how can we possibly organize a double-blind test? Should we randomly divide pupils in a class or school between different research conditions? Are we able to check group comparability in the same way that a pharmaceutical company can (for example, only people with a certain clinical profile and a certain age and/or weight, etc.)? Where will we find sufficiently large numbers of pupils to make this randomization possible? And what does it mean if something is statistically significant? As an illustration, the average effect size for life-saving interventions with medication (for example, the use of medicines to reduce blood pressure and therefore the incidence of strokes) is between 0.02 and 0.08, while the average size of effect for different educational interventions – based on a review of 302 meta-analyses containing more than 14,000 studies of educational and psychological interventions – amounts to 0.45.

With every medicine that you buy, you get a long leaflet that gives you lots of information about the circumstances in which the medicine will not work, when it is likely to have side-effects, and so on. Why do the pharmaceutical companies do this? Because the medicine is often targeted at a single specific condition, but it nonetheless has an impact on the body as a whole. Frequently, evidence-based education is also focused on a single specific approach, but if we look at the example of homework it is evident that many of the different elements in education interact with and influence each other: the impact of the learning-self, the home situation, the school context, the individual teachers, among others.

As a result, there is now a tendency in both medicine and education to no longer talk about evidence-based conclusions, but about *evidence-informed* conclusions. Woodbury and Kuhnke[14] defined this as follows for the medical profession: 'Evidence-informed practice (EIP) is a process for making informed clinical decisions. Research evidence is integrated with clinical experience, patient values, preferences and circumstances'. Translated into the educational field, this could be summarized as 'a research-informed approach, whereby the knowledge gained from scientific research is integrated into daily practice, so that well-considered choices can be made to reflect specific objectives and circumstances'.

Or to express it even more simply: the researchers have done fantastic work in recent decades to provide a huge amount of input for the education world, but they have not translated this input to meet the specific needs of your pupils and your classroom. The only person who can do this is you, the teacher, supported by the team around you. But to be able to do this effectively, both you and the team first need to have a good idea of what works, when and where, so that you can take well-considered and informed decisions based on scientific evidence that is relevant to your particular situation.

Fortunately, education possesses a number of advantages in this respect, when compared with medicine. For example, there are many more opportunities to experiment in education than in medicine, and people don't usually die in the classroom as a result – well, not often. But all joking aside, a teacher who realizes that a new approach is not working can quickly switch to a more successful alternative without any harm being done.

The question of whether an evidence-based or an evidence-informed approach is the best way forward is just one of the many conundrums in educational thinking at the present time. In this book I will be looking primarily at the 'how' aspect of the situation, at the didactics of education. I do this in the full realization that questions like 'what should we teach at school?' or 'what is the purpose of education?' are just as important, or even more important, than my focus on 'how do you achieve this?', but the pedagogic element will never be far away. In the following pages, for example, I will be looking at the importance of a good teacher–learner relationship, but I do not intend to enter into the complex curriculum content debate.

A plea for the informed amateur

Evidence-based or (better still) evidence-informed processes seem to form a good basis for the upgrading and revaluation of the teaching profession to the highest professional standards. A professional in any branch always has a set of effective tools at his or her disposal, which can be used in the right way and at the right moment, or else can be quickly substituted if things go wrong, so that if option A does not work, there is always an option B, C or even D. There is just one problem with this approach: in my experience, there are very few people in the teaching world who like referring to themselves as 'professionals' or who entered this world in the hope of acquiring such a status. Most people became teachers for the same simple reason: they wanted to do something with, and for, children.

In their book *Apologie van de school* [An apology for the school], Jan Masschelein and Maarten Simons[15] argue in favour of the need for more amateurism in education. At first, this may sound strange, particularly at a moment when we are hearing more and more about the need for greater professionalism. This is related to the fact that in some fields 'amateur' means more or less the same as 'incompetent'. But in other fields, an 'amateur' can be a fan, an enthusiast, a devotee or even a lover of something! This is the kind of 'amateur' we need more of in education. Just listen to the way most teachers talk about their charges: they invariably refer to 'my class', 'my students', 'my pupils'. This demonstrates a very high degree of personal commitment and deep sense of responsibility. This sense of responsibility and, by extension, the 'amateurism' of the teacher also means that when a teacher sees that a pupil is not making progress with the current approach, they will simply change that approach in the hope of finding a better way forward. As a responsible 'enthusiast', it is your task as a teacher to ensure that your pupils learn what they need to learn and to make this possible by augmenting your toolkit with options B, C and D, knowing in advance on the basis of your evidence-informed choices that these options have a good chance of working in your situation. Although when put like this, our amateur suddenly sounds quite professional, don't you think?

What this book is and is not

In light of the above, it should be clear that this book does not want to describe 'what works', but prefers to describe what often works, why it works and in which circumstances it works (for which target group). For example, we want to help you to understand why knowledge is important, but also how it can sometimes be a stumbling block in the learning process. With this in mind, we will examine why knowledge works and show you when and how best to use it.

Chapters will all follow more or less the same format. First, there will be a description of precisely what the approach or insight under discussion involves, followed by an assessment of why it is important, supplemented with different examples to illustrate when the approach or insight works well and when it might have more negative results. In this way, the book will shed light on the different ingredients you can use in the kitchen that is your classroom; not necessarily to turn every teacher into a masterchef, but to ensure that every dish – sorry, every lesson – is as good as it reasonably can be.

At the same time, the book is also an appeal to make more use of evidence-informed process in your teaching and to integrate the lessons contained in the following pages into your daily practice. It will not always be easy and sometimes you will experience setbacks. But never forget that for every failed lesson in the past, there are hundreds more in the future that will soon give you the opportunity to put things right.

To cut it short

- The same approach in education can generate big differences in effects.
- That is why it is better to work in ways that are evidence-informed rather than evidence-based.
- In evidence-informed education teachers use scientific insights to make deliberate choices that suit your own pupils or students.

Notes

1 Hattie, J. (2009). *Visible learning: A synthesis of over 800 meta-analyses relating to achievement*. Abingdon: Routledge; Hattie, J. (2012). *Visible learning for teachers: Maximizing impact on learning*. Abingdon: Routledge.

2 De Bruyckere, P., Kirschner, P.A., & Hulshof, C.D. (2015). *Urban myths about learning and education*. Cambridge, MA: Academic Press.

3 Willingham, D.T. (2012). *When can you trust the experts?: How to tell good science from bad in education*. Hoboken, NJ: John Wiley & Sons.

4 www-07.ibm.com/innovation/in/watson/watson_in_healthcare.html

5 www.ibm.com/watson/education/

6 www.wsj.com/articles/if-your-teacher-sounds-like-a-robot-you-might-be-on-to-something-1462546621

7 Clark, R.C., & Mayer, R.E. (2016). *E-learning and the science of instruction: Proven guidelines for consumers and designers of multimedia learning*. Hoboken, NJ: John Wiley & Sons.

8 Hattie, 2009.

9 There is some discussion about the effect sizes used by Hattie. On the one hand, some statisticians are sceptical about Hattie's specific use of the CLE measure (for a summary, see http://uv-net.uio.no/wpmu/lpu2/2012/02/11/kan-vi-stole-pa-hattiestatistikkbruk-i-utdanningsforskningen-iii-kommentar-fra-arne-kare-topphol/#comment-302). On the other hand, Dylan Wiliam rightly questions the use of effect sizes to compare different approaches. See: Wiliam, D. (2010). An integrative summary of the research literature and implications for a new theory of formative assessment. In H.L. Andrade & G.J. Cizek (Eds), *Handbook of formative assessment* (pp. 18–40). New York, NY: Taylor & Francis.

10 Cooper, H. (1989). *Homework*. White Plains, NY: Longman.

11 Marzano, R.J., & Pickering, D.J. (2007). Special topic: The case for and against homework. *Educational Leadership*, *64*(6), 74–79.

12 Castro, M., Expósito-Casas, E., López-Martín, E., Lizasoain, L., Navarro-Asencio, E., & Gaviria, J.L. (2015). Parental involvement on student academic achievement: a meta-analysis. *Educational Research Review*, *14*, 33–46.

13 Gravemeijer, K.P.E., & Kirschner, P.A. (2007). Naar meer evidence-based onderwijs? *Pedagogische Studiën*, *84*, 463–472.

14 Woodbury, M.G., & Kuhnke, J.L. (2014). What's the difference? *Wound Care Canada*, *12*(1).

15 Masschelein, J., & Simons, M. (2012). *Apologie van de school: Een publieke zaak* [In defense of the school: a public cause]. Leuven: Acco.

2

PRIOR KNOWLEDGE: HOW LEARNING BEGINS

This chapter will explore the following questions:

- Why is prior knowledge one of the most important preconditions for learning?
- What to do if a pupil or student doesn't have enough prior knowledge?
- What to do if a pupil or student has mistakes in his or her prior knowledge?

The spam-filter in our head

Let's begin this chapter with a little experiment, known as the Wason test. This test is in two parts. Good luck!

The first exercise is as follows:

Four cards are placed in front of you on a table. Each card has a letter on one side and a number on the other side. On the sides that you can see are the letters E and D and the numbers 4 and 7. You are now asked to check the validity of the following: 'For these four cards, the following rule applies: if there is a consonant on one side, there is an even number on the other side.' What is the minimum number of cards you need to turn over to see if this is true or not?

How many times did you read and re-read this exercise? And did you find the answer to the problem? The majority of the test subjects attempting to solve this conundrum set by Peter Wason say two cards: the E and the 4. But that is wrong. Before I explain why, you first get a chance to do better with the second part of the test:

You walk into a pub and you see the following four men:

- Someone drinking beer (man 1)
- Someone drinking cola (man 2)
- Someone who is 21 years old (man 3)
- Someone who is 16 years old (man 4)

Once again, you are asked to check the validity of a rule: 'If someone drinks beer, he must be older than 18 years of age'. How many and which of the men must you ask a minimal number of questions to see if the rule is true?

There is a significant likelihood that you will choose man 1 and man 4. According to Geake,[1] for the first task the majority of people, roughly 80%, incorrectly choose options 1 and 3, while for the second task an even larger majority, some 90%, choose options 1 and 4, which are correct. This, on the face of it, is strange, since the logic and the reasoning are exactly the same for both tasks.[2] But the first task seems much more difficult to work out than the second one.

What is the reason for this? The Wason experiment is an exercise to test our working memory. You have probably heard of the working memory as the memory which stores information for short periods of time in the brain (consequently, it is also sometimes called the short-term memory). The length of this storage can vary from just a few seconds to a few minutes, since the quantity of information that the working memory can store is limited.

As a result of research, we now know that the working memory also has another function. Geake describes this memory as a kind of spam-filter. We are constantly bombarded with countless different kinds of stimuli. The brain cannot process them all, and so is forced to make a selection. This selection is made in part by the working memory, which compares the stimuli with those that are already stored in the long-term memory. This is exactly the same way that a spam-filter checks if the addresses of your incoming mails are already known to you.

**FURTHER THINKING: WORKING MEMORY AND
SHORT-TERM MEMORY: SYNONYMS?**

In the above text, I (like many people) use the terms 'working memory' and 'short-term memory' almost interchangeably. Yet in reality they are not synonyms. Aben, Stapert and Blokland[3] make the following distinction: 'The theoretical-conceptual short-term memory and the working memory refer respectively to storage and the storage and processing of information'. In concrete terms, the main difference is that the working memory does more than simply store information, which is all that the short-term memory can do. The working memory actually combines and/or modifies this information. If we think back to our spam-filter analogy, this filter also manipulates information: in other words, it compares information with what you already know. That is why from now on I will use the term 'working memory' for the rest of the book.

Why is prior information important?

What are the consequences of having this spam-filter in our head? It makes clear that prior information is important when selecting new information to absorb and also demonstrates that this new knowledge can best be embedded in 'old' knowledge that the learner already possesses. David Ausbel stated 'that if I have to reduce all educational psychology to just one principle, I would say this: "the most important single factor influencing learning is what the learner already knows." Ascertain this and teach him accordingly'.[4]

It costs you much greater effort to digest information you don't recognize than information you do recognize, which is why the first task in the Wason test was so much harder. The spam-filter is also the reason why, in most cases, it is best to first present pupils in the classroom with something concrete to absorb, before attempting to move on to new insights or the development of existing ones.

This confirms a number of the older tenets of didactic theory. During my own training (now some years ago), I also received instruction in the principle of examples,[5] for which De Block argues that it is better for teachers to move from concrete illustrations via schematic arrangement to abstract concepts. This can easily be understood by looking at how a child learns about the number 4.

Step 1 is to show the child four apples. Step 2 is to show the child a schematic arrangement of four dots. Step 3 is to show the child the figure 4, which by itself, does little to remind us that it represents something consisting of four elements. For the sake of clarity, I should also point out that these three steps I have just described can each take some time for the child to absorb.

If we talk about presenting something concrete or visual examples, this does not mean by definition we need to use physical objects that children can touch and smell. In the example of the Wason test at the start of this chapter, the test subjects did not physically go to a pub, nor did Wason hire four actors to play the roles in his test centre. Instead, he simply created a mental image that everyone could easily picture.

There is another related process which also seems to be confirmed by this insight; namely, that you should take the personal environment of the learner as the starting point for your teaching, in the sense that you should relate what you are trying to teach to things that the pupil is already familiar with. That being said, later in the chapter we will see that this is not always a good idea and that 'prior information' and 'environment' are not necessarily synonyms.

FURTHER THINKING: ONE OF THE OLDEST DIDACTIC PRINCIPLES: RELATE YOUR TEACHING TO THE ENVIRONMENT OF THE LEARNER

This didactic recommendation is nothing new. As early as the beginning of the 20th century, Decroly was already referring to 'centres of interest', meaning subjects from the environment of the pupils that can be used to develop learning activities; for example, in nursery schools.[6] In 1954, Aarts formulated this thinking into what he called 'the founding principle of didactics': namely, that 'all education must be rooted in the child's own personal history'. By this, Aarts meant that the things offered to the children as learning aids during their education should relate to the environment and surroundings in which those children had grown up. This is often referred to in the Anglo-Saxon literature as 'the situated nature of learning' (although this can mean either connecting with the child's environment or connecting with the course of studies that you are teaching).[7] By arguing in favour of the need for a clear connection with the child's background and surroundings, the further connection to motivation is quickly made. Connecting with the learner's environment is therefore the basis for more easily engaging the pupil's attention and for motivating him or her intrinsically.[8]

Choosing the right situational methods for Ann and David

Let me introduce you to Ann and David. They are both in my class and their IQ tests suggest that their level of intelligence is comparable. Putting it crudely, they are both as smart as each other. Ann comes from an averagely well-off family, and his parents have already taken him to see the Coliseum in Rome and the Acropolis in Athens. In contrast, David comes from a family with a low social-economic status and he has never been outside his home town. It is not difficult to guess which of the two would have an advantage in a lesson about classical antiquity. Ann has much more prior information on this subject and will therefore be able to much more easily link new insights to his own experiences, whereas David will find this much more difficult.

In their work, Hattie and Yates[9] made a comparison between two different methods of pupil engagement: (self-)discovery learning versus direct instruction. They also compared the effect of the different methods on learning and well-being. The methods differ significantly from each other, particularly in the extent to which the teacher gives guidance to the pupil (with plenty of guidance in direct instruction and much less in discovery learning). In the following paragraphs, I will discuss the consequences of prior information for both methods, as an illustration of the importance of teacher guidance when the learner has insufficient or inaccurate prior knowledge.

FURTHER THINKING: WHAT IS DIRECT INSTRUCTION AND WHAT IS (SELF-)DISCOVERY LEARNING?

It is often very difficult to delineate the definition of concepts in education. Veenman[10] has argued that four different things can be meant by the term 'direct instruction':

- Methods of education in which the learning activities of the pupil are regulated by the teacher (generally known as teacher-led instruction);

- Methods of instruction that have evolved out of research into what makes an effective teacher (so-called process-product research);

(Continued)

- Methods of instruction that have evolved out of research into the learning of cognitive strategies (cognitive strategy instruction);

- Methods of instruction that have developed out of special education programmes for pupils with learning difficulties, such as the DISTAR programme (Direct Instruction Systems in Arithmetic and Reading).

What these four descriptions have in common is the strong and leading role played by the teacher. In short, and harking back to the starting points postulated by Siegfried Engelmann and Wesley Becker who originally developed the model, you can assume that in direction instruction the teacher will give detailed explanations of how a particular learning task should be carried out. The pupil is given examples and is shown exactly how the different steps in the process should be performed. In this way, the task is demonstrated systematically for the pupil, almost step by step. Once this has been done, the pupil is left to his or her own devices.[11] Direct instruction first became widely known through the world-famous Project Follow Through, which was probably the largest and most expensive educational experiment of all time, conducted between 1968 and 1977 in the United States. The project compared different approaches to education and teaching, with the direct instruction model proving to be one of the most effective.[12]

The terms '(self-)discovery learning' or 'discovery-based learning' can also mean a number of different things, and there are now even several variants, such as enquiry-based learning. Discovery learning dates back to the theories developed by Jerome Bruner,[13] who in turn was inspired by, amongst others, the work of Jean Piaget and his belief that a child was an active processor of knowledge. The essential starting point for the discovery learning method is that the learner guides himself, or herself, through the learning process. This means that the pupil does not receive all the necessary information in neat little chunks from the teachers, as is the case in direct instruction, but needs instead to make the necessary effort to find, sort and arrange this information in a new order. The purpose of discovery learning is therefore to develop problem-solving capabilities.

One of the good things about discovery learning is its effect on the pupil's state of mind: most of them like this freer approach, so that their sense of well-being increases. But this 'feel-good' factor comes at a price: the gulf between the good students and bad students is much greater with this method. This is not difficult to understand, if we think back to the example of Ann and David. However, the gulf between the strong and the weak learners is a lot smaller with direct instruction, not because Ann performs worse, but because David performs better. But this better performance again comes at a price: their sense of well-being will be lower.

Hattie and Yates summarize this as follows:

> For instance, several studies have found that low ability students will prefer discovery learning lessons to direct-instruction-based lessons, but learn less from them. Under conditions of low guidance, the knowledge gap between low and high ability students tends to increase. The lack of direct guidance has greater damaging effects on learning in low ability students especially when procedures are unclear, feedback is reduced, and misconceptions remain as problems to be resolved rather than errors to be corrected.[14]

It is already bad enough if learning opportunities are lost through a lack of prior knowledge, which means that pupils are unable to extract what they potentially should from the examples, texts or images that are available to them. It is even worse when deficient prior knowledge creates a negative learning effect, because pupils find it difficult to assess whether what they are reading is accurate or not. In these circumstances, something can still be learned, but the related information and insights are generally wrong. We will see shortly that these errors can often be stubborn and persistent.

On the basis of this comparison between direct instruction and discovery learning, we can draw a number of interesting conclusions:

- **Well-being and learning are *not* synonymous**. If they occur together, that's fine. But it is important to remember that the two concepts are not linked in a positive manner *per se*.
- **Variation in working methods is crucial**. If you only use discovery learning, the gap in knowledge between your most able and your least able pupils will grow, although they will probably all feel happy and contented. If you only use direct instruction, your pupils will most likely make good progress more uniformly, although some may drop out because they no longer feel comfortable with the method of teaching used.

There is little likelihood in this day and age that a school will confine itself to just a single method of teaching, although educational history gives us some examples of this from the not-too-distant past. But when exactly should you apply direct instruction and when is it better to choose discovery learning?

To answer this question, it is important to realize that there are different types of knowledge and different learning objectives. Leaving aside the multiplicity of distinctions between different kinds of knowledge and goals that exist nowadays, I would like to focus on a simple distinction between basic knowledge and basic objectives, the fundamentals that everyone must be taught; and deeper insights and objectives, which can only be realized once you have mastered the basics (or to put it another way, when you have the correct prior information).

If we look at the difference between direct instruction and discovery learning specifically in terms of basic knowledge, it is clear that direct instruction scores much better. It is not until pupils possess this indispensable prior knowledge that they will be able to start learning on their own.

FURTHER THINKING: PERHAPS THE MOST IMPORTANT GRAPHIC FROM PISA 2015

In December 2016, the OECsD published the most recent PISA results, which looked at the academic performance of 15-year-old students in the participating countries for subjects including mathematics, language and sciences. In particular, attention was focused on the latter discipline and the graphic contained in the report's conclusions (Figure 2.1) was, in my opinion, highly significant (I have added the two boxed frames myself).

This graphic contains both a 'to-do' list of things that need to be improved (such as socio-economic status and gender inequality) and a 'how-to' list that assesses the best methods to achieve the right results. In this latter respect, it is noticeable that enquiry-based instruction (i.e. discovery learning) results in much lower levels of performance than teacher-directed instruction. This is striking, because at first sight it runs contrary to what we most frequently hear in current education circles about the best way to teach STEM subjects. However, we must be careful not to misinterpret these figures: it is not as simple as saying: 'Okay, so let's just use traditional education methods'. This is not what the figures say and it is certainly not what the people behind PISA would recommend. Look, for example, at the good score achieved by adaptive (i.e. online, computer-based) instruction. It is evident that what we really need is differentiated education.

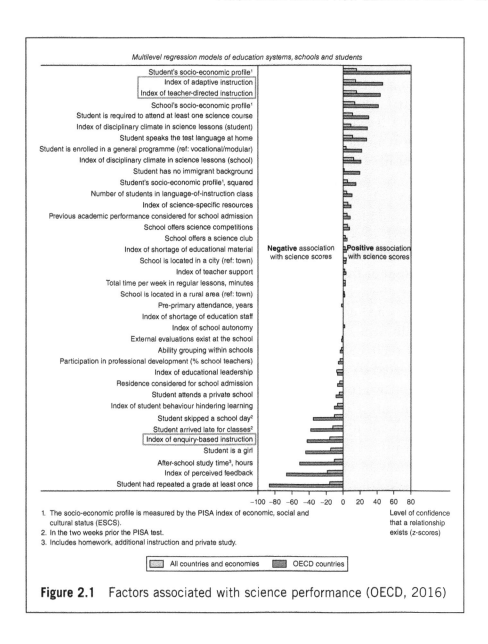

Figure 2.1   Factors associated with science performance (OECD, 2016)

How can we make a valid choice between teaching methods in terms of the pupil's prior knowledge?

In concrete terms, it is necessary for teachers to make a well-considered choice between the two teaching methods of direct instruction and discovery learning:

1. Decide what prior knowledge the pupils need to follow a new lesson or to explore the relevant themes themselves.
2. Try to assess the extent to which individual pupils possess the required prior knowledge (or not).
3. Adopt a teacher-based approach (for example, direct instruction) to brush up the required prior knowledge of the pupils who do not possess it, so that they will then be capable of working on their own.

How can you translate these basic instructions into practice? Here is a simple example. After you have decided what prior knowledge your pupils need, choose five core words or insights that they should already know if they possess this knowledge. The pupils who can describe four or five of the core concepts with relative ease can immediately be allowed to explore the subject of the lesson by themselves. For pupils who know three core words (or perhaps even four, but still don't really feel confident), you should provide a short text that refreshes their memory of the themes involved (this text is sometimes referred to as an advanced organizer). The pupils who know just one or two (or even none) of the words need to be taken aside and given direct instruction by the teacher, so that they can then work independently later on in the lesson, once they have gained the necessary prior knowledge. Remember, however, that we are talking here (by way of example) about two rather extreme points in the didactic spectrum: direct instruction and discovery learning. There are many other didactic methods between these extremes that can be usefully employed, depending on the circumstances.

FURTHER THINKING: WHAT IS AN ADVANCED ORGANIZER?

An advanced organizer is a concept first developed by David Ausubel.[15] It is a small text or drawing containing relevant key information that is given to the pupils before the start of a learning process. In this way, the prior knowledge necessary for the process is 'freshened up' in the pupils' minds, so that they can more easily deal with and organize any new information with which they are confronted in the course of the lesson. Advanced organizers are particularly beneficial for pupils with little prior knowledge of the subject involved.

What if the prior knowledge contains errors?

Until now, we have focused on the difference between pupils with sufficient and insufficient prior knowledge. But what happens if the prior knowledge possessed by students is not (wholly) correct?[16] In this respect, there are different gradations of error.[17] The worst of these is when a pupil has learnt something that is wrong and thereafter continues to learn on the basis of inaccurate prior knowledge. When this happens, it can be very difficult to unlearn something that has been incorrectly learnt. This is because the pupil will already have repeated the error time after time in their head, so that the status of the incorrect knowledge has been 'confirmed'. This might also explain why the myth of learning styles is so persistent amongst teaching staff... but don't despair: very difficult does not mean impossible.

Some other situations are not quite so bad. As a teacher, you have probably had learners who see an analogy incorrectly. A variation of this is when a pupil uses a technique that they have learnt somewhere else, even though that technique is not relevant to what is being taught today. In one sense, it is good that the pupil has tried to transfer and apply prior knowledge to a different situation, but it is obviously unfortunate that on this occasion it is the wrong situation. In these circumstances, it is important that the pupil is explicitly shown that the analogy he or she believes to be right is, in fact, wrong. Above, all, they must be helped to understand why it is wrong.

What can the teacher – and the learner – do about these errors? Research conducted in 2012 at Duke University proved that it is possible to correct ingrained errors by giving repeated feedback, which the researchers referred to as hypercorrection. The results indicated that if learners answered a test question incorrectly, they were more likely to remember the right answer later on if they were demonstrably corrected. And the more certain the learners were about the accuracy of their original answer, the more likely they were to remember the correction. However, the researchers also established that in most cases this was only true for a short time. The likelihood that the error would return in the long-term, once the correction had been forgotten, was significantly higher.

How can this be prevented? According to Butler et al.,[18] it is important to give pupils and students enough exercises that require them to extract the right answers from their store of prior knowledge. The more frequently they are required to recall the right information, the greater the probability that they will avoid wrong information.

The danger of focusing on the learner's personal environment

It is important that we continue to make a distinction between a pupil's personal environment and prior knowledge. Wherein lies the difference? The term 'personal environment' refers explicitly to all the things that exist in the life of a child or young person. The term 'prior knowledge' describes knowledge about a particular subject that is present in the child's or young person's memory and can be used as a basis for further development. A simple example will serve to clarify this point. In a lesson about transport, the teacher may ask: 'Who has flown in a plane?' This question relates to the pupil's personal environment, whereas a possible alternative question, 'What is a plane?', probes the child's prior knowledge about the concept 'plane'.[19]

While it may seem logical to take the pupil's personal environment as a starting point for learning, since this will connect more readily with what the pupil already knows and will make it easier to bypass their inbuilt spam-filter, there are nonetheless two possible dangers associated with this approach.

Remaining too long in the personal environment

The purpose of education is to open up the world to children. If, as a teacher, you focus too long on the child's narrow personal environment, there is a danger that he or she might lose interest, because they are not being fascinated or challenged by anything new. To make matters worse, it is also a negation of all the most important educational responsibilities.

Gert Biesta summarizes these responsibilities as subjectification, socialization and qualification. Biesta has written extensively on these matters, but in essence he is referring to 1) personal development, 2) learning to live in a society where the child can make the customs and tradition of the community his or her own and 3) the acquisition of knowledge, skills and attitudes that make it possible to do things. This latter element, qualification, can either be very specific (for example, educating a pupil to follow a particular profession) or more general (preparing young people to live in a complex, multicultural society). This leads to the conclusion that education is fundamentally a question of first connecting with a child in their personal environment, and then opening up that environment to the world.

Narrower mental bandwidth as a result of the personal environment

In 2013, Mani et al.[20] published research findings in *Science* relating to their investigation of the link between specific intelligence and poverty. In particular, the researchers examined the negative effect that poverty can have on a person's intellectual capabilities. This required them to move away from the idea that intelligence is fixed. They concluded that concerns about poverty can have a negative impact on IQ by no fewer than 12 to 13 points. This is comparable with taking an intelligence test on the morning after 'a night on the town', as demonstrated by Mullainathan and Shafir in their book *Scarcity*.[21]

On the basis of this research, behavioural economist Mullainathan and psychologist Shafir further developed a new theory based on the impact of scarcity on our thinking and actions. This involves much more than just the effects of poverty. It also covers other forms of scarcity, such as the lack of time experienced by an overworked employee.

Together with Maarten Simons, I explored the possible consequences of these conclusions for education. Mullainathan and Shafir referred in their findings to tests they had conducted with the children of air traffic controllers. They established that during busy and stressful periods at work, when the controllers' mental bandwidth was devoted exclusively to their job, the controllers' children were treated more negatively at home. They similarly established that towards the end of any given month children living in poverty were also treated more negatively, as their parents struggled to cope with the pressure of surviving financially until the next payday (which, like the controllers, significantly reduced their mental bandwidth). These are just two of the many examples of the way in which a child's personal environment can sometimes have a negative impact on their ability to learn. However, the research designs used by Mullainathan and Shafir to reach their conclusions also reveal other dangers that can emanate from the need to use the personal environment as the starting point for the child's learning. For example, what if this environment also puts the mental bandwidth of the child under pressure? We already know from cognitive overload theory that bad life conditions (such as stress or anxiety) can hamper the ability to learn.[22] Mullainathan and Shafir[23] noted that when they 'forced' their test subjects to think about their personal situation, this had an immediate negative effect on their intellectual performance. The reverse was also true; if they were allowed to forget about their circumstances, performance improved.

The key question for education is, therefore, to what extent seeking to connect with a child's personal environment can actually narrow that child's mental bandwidth, rather than broadening it? This will undoubtedly vary from child to child. Nor should we forget that any child's personal environment will be much more than just cares and woes. Even so, Mullainathan and Shafir argue that situations of scarcity can become mentally overpowering, so that people, children included, can develop a kind of tunnel vision. For example, someone on a diet is probably always thinking about food. In the same way, someone living in poverty is always thinking, often involuntarily, about their precarious situation.

This connects with the description by Masschelein and Simons[24] of school as being 'a liberator' and possibly even 'an equalizer' (my words, based on Masschelein and Simons). Children come to school and school makes them equal, albeit temporarily, in their joint status as 'pupils', in a manner which takes no account of, and therefore liberates them from, their background and environment. In this respect, school is a place where children can forget their personal worries, even if only for a short time. Viewed from the scarcity perspective, this can have a positive effect on learning.

To cut it short

- Prior knowledge assists learning if the knowledge is sufficiently present, appropriate and correct.
- Prior knowledge hinders learning if the knowledge is not sufficiently present, not appropriate and/or not correct.
- It is important for the teacher to establish what prior knowledge the pupils need, to assess what level of prior knowledge the individual pupils already possess and, where necessary, to enhance that prior knowledge, so that all the pupils will later be capable of working more independently.
- It can sometimes be beneficial to connect with the pupil's personal environment, but not for too long, since this environment can sometimes also be harmful.

Notes

1 Geake, J. (2009). *The brain at school: Educational neuroscience in the classroom*. London: McGraw-Hill Education (UK).
2 The rule was '*If* there is a consonant on one side, *then* there is an even number on the other side'. Only a card with both a consonant on one face *and* something other than an even number on the other face can invalidate this rule.
3 Aben, B., Stapert, S., & Blokland, A. (2013). Kortetermijngeheugen en werkgeheugen: Zinnig of dubbelzinnig? *Tijdschrift voor neuropsychologie, 8(2)*.
4 Ausubel, D.P., Novak, J.D., & Hanesian, H. (1968). *Educational psychology: A cognitive view*. New York: Holt, Rinehart and Winston Inc.
5 See: De Block, A., & Heene, J. (1986). *Inleiding tot de algemene didactiek*. Standard; De Block, A., & Heene, J. (1993). *De School en haar doelstellingen*. Antwerpen: Standard Educatieve Uitgeverij.
6 Decroly, O., & Boon, G. (1921). *Vers l'école rénovée: une première étape*. Paris: Librairie Fernand Nathan.
7 Driscoll, M.P. (2000). *Psychology for instruction*. London: Pearson.
8 Schuit, H., de Vrieze, I., & Sleegers, P. (2011). *Leerlingen motiveren: een onderzoek naar de rol van leraren* (Vol. 27). Ruud de Moor Centrum/ Open Universiteit.
9 Hattie, J., & Yates, G.C. (2013). *Visible Learning and the science of how we learn*. Abingdon: Routledge.

10 Veenman S. (2001), *Directe instructie*. Paper written for the course in Instruction Skills at the *Sectie Onderwijs en Educatie* at the Catholic University of Nijmegen.

11 Bakermans J., Franzen Y., Hoof N. van, Veenman S., & Boer G. de (1997). *Effectieve instructie in het voortgezet onderwijs. Leren onderwijzen met behulp van het directe instructiemodel.* Amersfoort, CPS.

12 Evans, J.H. (1981). *What have we learned from Follow Through? Implications for future R & D programs.* Washington DC, National Institute of Education (ERIC Document Reproduction Service No. ED244737).

13 Bruner, J. (1972). *Play: Its role in development and evolution.* Harmondsworth: Penguin.

14 Hattie & Yates, 2013, p. 114.

15 Ausubel, D.P. (1960). The use of advance organizers in the learning and retention of meaningful verbal material. *Journal of Educational Psychology, 51,* 267–272.

16 Alvermann, D.E., Smith, L.C., & Readence, J.E. (1985). Prior knowledge activation and the comprehension of compatible and incompatible text. *Reading Research Quarterly, 20,* 420–436.

17 Ambrose, S.A., Bridges, M.W., DiPietro, M., Lovett, M.C., & Norman, M.K. (2010). *How learning works: Seven research-based principles for smart teaching.* Hoboken, NJ: John Wiley & Sons.

18 Butler, A.C., Fazio, L.K., & Marsh, E.J. (2011). The hypercorrection effect persists over a week, but high-confidence errors return'. *Psychonomic Bulletin & Review, 18*(6), 1238–1244.

19 De Bruyckere, P., & Simons, M. (2016). Scarcity at school. *European Educational Research Journal, 15*(2), 260–267.

20 Mani, A., Mullainathan, S., Shafir, E., & Zhao, J. (2013). Poverty impedes cognitive function. *Science, 341*(6149), 976–980.

21 Mullainathan, S., & Shafir, E. (2013). *Scarcity: Why having too little means so much.* Basingstoke: Macmillan.

22 Hattie & Yates, 2013.

23 Mullainathan & Shafir, 2013.

24 Masschelein & Simons, 2012.

3

THE SUBJECT MATTER KNOWLEDGE OF THE TEACHER

This chapter will explore the following questions:

- Why is the subject matter knowledge of the teacher important?
- Why doesn't more subject matter knowledge automatically lead to better teachers?
- What is the 'curse of knowledge' and how can you bypass it?

In the previous chapter we saw just how important prior knowledge can be for influencing the learning ability of pupils and students. But what about the subject matter knowledge of the teachers? Because you are trying to teach things to your pupils and students, it stands to reason that you should first know what you are talking about. This might sound like stating the obvious, but the situation is not always as straightforward as it might seem. For example, in the often heated discussions about the best methods of teaching and learning, some of the protagonists have even gone so far as to say that a teacher requires no subject matter knowledge whatsoever,[1] but should simply 'coach' the learners through their learning process. This is clearly taking things too far, but it does not necessarily mean that those who argue in favour of more subject matter knowledge for teachers are always in the right.

At a recent researchED[2] conference in Amsterdam, Professor Daniel Muijs summarized the situation as follows: 'There is no simple, linear connection between the knowledge possessed by the teacher and the resultant learning ability of the pupils'. This is the kind of statement that can easily be misunderstood. I have also witnessed equally surprised reactions to the contention of John Hattie[3] in his analysis of educational meta-analyses that more subject matter knowledge only has a very small effect on pupil learning ability.

Some clarification is necessary. What these authors in their different ways are most certainly *not* saying is that subject matter knowledge is unimportant in teaching and learning. The crucial word in Professor Muijs's statement is 'linear'. If such a linear connection did exist, this would mean that the acquisition of more subject matter knowledge by a teacher would automatically be reflected in his or her performance and the pupils' learning results. However, this is self-evidently not the case.

I am sure that, like me, you have sometimes listened to an expert speaker and thought: 'Gosh, she's clever, but I can't understand a word she's saying!' This leads to the question: have you actually learnt anything from that clever expert? Hattie and Jaeger[4] refer to the need for more expert teachers rather than experts. Personally, I prefer to speak of the teacher as a translator, the person who decodes and adapts content and objectives, before communicating them to the learners. To be able to do this successfully, it is beyond dispute that you need teachers with a sufficient degree of subject matter knowledge. In this chapter we will look at two of the more unexpected benefits of this sufficient subject matter knowledge, but also at two of the potential dangers that may arise when the teacher has too much professional background knowledge. And rest assured: I will not be making any plea to ignore lesson content, but I will be attempting to make you more aware of the so-called 'curse of knowledge'.

FURTHER THINKING: DIFFICULT WORDS DON'T MAKE YOU SEEM ANY SMARTER

If you are a speaker, it is obviously of vital importance that the people listening to you can understand what you are saying. There is no point in blinding your audience with the eloquence of your words. Nowhere is this truer than in the classroom, otherwise you run the risk that the pupils will stop listening. While research has shown that intelligent people are more inclined to use difficult words,[5] it is ironic to note that other research suggests that the use of difficult words makes you seem less intelligent! In three simple experiments, Daniel Oppenheimer has demonstrated that fluent texts with simple language are more positively assessed by readers.[6] This does not mean that you should never learn jargon or must eliminate difficult words from your vocabulary. But the more easily a reader or listener is able to digest your message, the more highly you will be regarded as a speaker or writer.

How can you best use your subject matter knowledge in the classroom?

As I have already mentioned, it is logical that a teacher should know more about the teaching profession than the pupils they teach. However, it is difficult to estimate exactly how much more. The answer? Put simply: enough so that the teacher feels sufficiently confident to no longer worry about lesson content. But as a translator, there is one other thing the teacher needs that is even more important: the ability to process content and present it at the level of the pupil.

For example, it is essential to realize that a beginner needs to be addressed differently from an expert.[7] Learning how to ride a bike requires a different form of practice and concentration than preparing to take part as an experienced cyclist in the Tour De France. Similarly, people who don't like blues music often say that the genre is monotone and repetitive, a complaint that non-dance lovers likewise make about electronic dance music. But the fans of these genres usually fail to understand the criticisms, because they can see layers of nuance that others are unable to see, transforming blues and dance – for them at least – to a higher musical plane.

Scaffolding: the right support and the right time

The fact that beginners learn differently from experts reflects the complex learning trajectory that learners, and their teachers, must follow. In their recent book *Peak*, Anders Ericsson and Robert Pool[8] claim that repetitive practice by itself is not enough to build up expertise. Learners need the right support in their learning process at the right time. This refers back to what we saw in the previous chapter about the importance for teachers to monitor the existing levels of prior knowledge among their individual pupils or students. To this we can now add that teachers also need to adjust their lesson content and approach to match those levels of knowledge.

Many teachers will probably feel instinctively that they recognize the diagram below (Figure 3.1), since this is what they do most of the time: connect with what is known in the literature as 'the zone of proximal development'. This concept was first described by Vygotsky,[9] who argued that teachers must seek to interact with their learners at a level just beyond a learner's reach.[10] This means at a

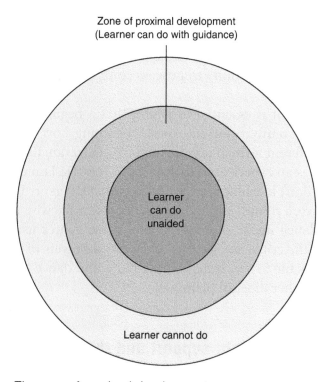

Figure 3.1　The zone of proximal development

level that the learner is capable of understanding and can actually achieve with a little extra effort and guidance. For example, if Margaret can already count to 100, with a bit of a push she should be able to count up to 1000. But if the challenge is too easy, she will lose interest. This is also the case if the challenge is too difficult. By continually finding new challenges at the right level, teachers are able to build a kind of platform that the learners can climb; hence the use of the term 'scaffolding'.[11] This makes clear just how important the role of the teacher, or the 'more knowledgeable other', really is. Without the teacher's input, the learner can never know what the next suitable challenge should be.

FURTHER THINKING: ZONE OF PROXIMAL DEVELOPMENT, ZONE OF PROXIMAL LEARNING OR RATHER SCAFFOLDING?

Vygotsky is well-known for his zone of proximal development, but Palincsar[12] called it 'probably one of the most used and least understood constructs to appear in contemporary educational literature'. And I have to admit that I also misunderstood this zone of proximal development until Dylan Wiliam pointed out on Twitter that there is something peculiar about the name of this infamous theory.

Vygotsky is talking about development, not about zone of proximal learning. And this isn't a mistake. The famous Russian educational thinker wrote 'the distance between the actual developmental level as determined by independent problem solving and the level of potential development as determined through problem solving under adult guidance or in collaboration with more capable peers'.[13]

Chaiklin[14] explains why this is: when discussing the zone of proximal development Vygotsky was not concerned with the development of skill of any particular task, but he argued that it must be related to development. Therefore Chaiklin concludes:

It seems more appropriate to use the term zone of proximal development to refer to the phenomenon that Vygotsky was writing about, and find other terms (e.g., assisted instruction, scaffolding) to refer to practices like teaching a specific subject-matter concept, skill, and so forth.

Subject matter knowledge as a minimum requirement for class management

One of the biggest worries of beginning teachers is how they will manage to control their class. There are many tips and tricks to make this possible and they are all necessary, because running an effective class is a serious challenge. But there is one important aspect that is often overlooked: a successful teacher also needs to possess sufficient subject matter knowledge.

What does subject matter knowledge have to do with class management? Why is it an important precondition for keeping your class under control? Consider the following scenario. Imagine you are going to see your favourite band. On the way, you suddenly ask yourself whether you remembered to turn the gas off. There is nobody at home you can call. None of the neighbours can check for you (they haven't got a key). How much do you think you are going to enjoy the concert in these circumstances? Probably not as much as you would like. Being worried about something reduces what Mullainathan and Shafir[15] call mental bandwidth. This means that you are less able to concentrate on whatever you are doing. Now imagine that you are uncertain about the lesson content you need to give to your next class. Perhaps there are some things where you hope that the pupils won't ask too many difficult questions, because if they do... When this happens, the mental bandwidth you need to keep the class under control is used up instead by your uncertainty about your own knowledge and ability. Viewed in these terms, working to improve your subject matter knowledge is a way to develop the mental calm that will allow you to manage the pupils and give your lesson properly.

FURTHER THINKING: THE IMPOSTER SYNDROME

Sometimes you will feel frightened. Frightened that one day someone will suddenly tap you on the shoulder and tell you that they can see through your masquerade. They know it's all just an act; that you are only pretending to know everything. In reality, you are a fraud, a cheat, a phoney...

When this happens, there are just two possibilities: either they are right (in which case you are in the wrong job) or else you are the victim of imposter syndrome. The good news? You are not alone.[16] Even more importantly, there are things that can help: the realization that it is just a syndrome, having a good mentor, talking it through with colleagues, learning to appreciate the value of your own hard work, are all ways to overcome these fears.

Subject matter knowledge as an element in the relationship between pupils and teachers

What are the things that ensure that pupils see their teacher as someone who is authentic? That was the subject of my own doctoral thesis.[17] We discovered several criteria. To be regarded as a 'real' teacher, pupils first and foremost expect passion from the person standing at the front of the class. This means someone who lives for his or her profession, but without taking this to idiotic extremes. Pupils also expect uniqueness and individuality, which can best be expressed by adjusting your lessons to suit the needs of individual pupils and individual classes. Equally important is knowing how to establish the right degree of distance and proximity with the pupils; not too close, but not too remote either. This means that pupils don't want you to try and be their friend, but they do want you to show an interest in their lives; preferably, in more informal moments during activities away from the classroom.

I have saved the most important criterion for last. The majority of the pupils questioned in our research said that the truest sign of a 'real' teacher was subject matter knowledge. Pupils want to learn, which means that the teacher has to know what he or she is doing. Not necessarily as an all-seeing instructor; more as a kind of translator-guide. In this way, subject matter knowledge can become a key element in the pupil–teacher relationship.

When can subject matter knowledge hinder learning?

You have probably heard some teachers say: 'It seems as though my pupils are getting more stupid each year'. Of course, you would never dream of saying this, but you may have heard a colleague say something like this. So what is going on? It seems likely that your colleagues are suffering from what is known as 'the curse of knowledge'.

What is this curse? It is actually an error in reasoning, often referred to as a cognitive bias, which means that when you are talking with someone you unconsciously assume that this person has the same background, views, convictions, and so on, as you do and will therefore automatically understand what you are saying.[18] Or as Carl Wieman[19] once put it: 'It is the idea that when you know something, it is extremely difficult to think about it from the perspective of someone who does not know it'. In terms of the classroom, it means that the teacher has become estranged from his translating role and has reverted to being an instructor *pursang*. Teachers often give the same subject to the same age group year after year. After a while, they develop a higher and higher degree of expertise, whereas the pupils remain at the same much lower level. As a result, the gulf between the teacher's knowledge and the pupils' knowledge gets wider and wider. At the same time, the teacher's temper can get shorter and shorter, because the pupils keep on asking the same 'stupid' questions (the teacher forgets that for them this is all new). So if you know colleagues who feel this way, or if you feel this way yourself, perhaps the moment has come to think about changing subject, changing class or even changing job.

FURTHER THINKING: IS SUBJECT MATTER SIMILARLY IMPORTANT FOR DIFFERENT SUBJECTS?

In the research on effectiveness of teaching, and also wider school effectiveness, there has been a shift in thinking acknowledging that good teaching can be different depending on different contexts.[20] This is also the case for how important subject matter is. Some major studies on teacher effectiveness commissioned by the British Teacher Training Agency showed, for example, that subject knowledge mattered less in teaching numeracy than in teaching literacy.[21]

To cut it short

- There is no linear connection between the level of a teacher's subject matter knowledge and the learning ability of pupils.
- Subject matter knowledge is an important prerequisite for successful class management and a fruitful teacher–pupil relationship.
- A teacher must know what he or she is talking about, but must also be able to translate this to the different levels of knowledge in the pupils they teach.
- If the gulf in expertise between the teacher and the pupils becomes too great, the former may fall victim to 'the curse of knowledge' to the detriment of the latter.

Notes

1 Dolmans, D.H., Gijselaers, W.H., Moust, J.H., Grave, W.S.D., Wolfhagen, I.H., & Vleuten, C.P.V.D. (2002). Trends in research on the tutor in problem-based learning: conclusions and implications for educational practice and research. *Medical Teacher*, 24(2), 173–180.

2 Muijs, D. (2016). *Leraareffectiviteit?Wat weten we (niet)?* researchED Amsterdam.

3 Hattie, 2009, 2012; Hattie, J. (2015). The applicability of Visible Learning to higher education. *Scholarship of Teaching and Learning in Psychology*, 1(1), 79–91.

4 Hattie J., & Jaeger, R. (1998). Assessment and classroom learning: a deductive approach. *Assessment in Education: Principles, Policy & Practice*, 5(1), 111–122.

5 Pennebaker, J.W., & King L.A. (1999). Linguistic styles: language use as an individual difference. *Journal of Personality and Social Psychology*, 77(6), 1296.

6 Oppenheimer, D.M. (2006). Consequences of erudite vernacular utilized irrespective of necessity: problems with using long words needlessly. *Applied Cognitive Psychology*, 20(2), 139–156.

7 Willingham, D.T. (2009). *Why don't students like school? A cognitive scientist answers questions about how the mind works and what it means for the classroom.* Hoboken, NJ: John Wiley and Sons.

8 Ericsson, A., & Pool, R. (2016). *Peak: Secrets from the new science of expertise.* Boston, MA: Houghton Mifflin Harcourt.

9 Chaiklin, S. (2003). The zone of proximal development in Vygotsky's analysis of learning and instruction. *Vygotsky's Educational Theory in Cultural Context*, *1*, 39–64.

10 Well, it's often understood and quoted like this, but if this is correct, check the Further Thinking box...

11 Wood, D., Bruner, J.S., & Ross, G. (1976). The role of tutoring in problem-solving. *Journal of Child Psychology and Psychiatry*, *17*(2), 89–100.

12 Palincsar, A.S. (1998). Keeping the metaphor of scaffolding fresh – a response to C. Addison Stone's 'The metaphor of scaffolding: Its utility for the field of learning disabilities'. *Journal of Learning Disabilities*, *31*(4), 370–373.

13 Vygotsky, L. (1978). Interaction between learning and development. *Readings on the Development of Children*, *23*(3), 79–91. This reference is to p. 86, emphasis in the original.

14 Chaiklin, 2003.

15 Mullainathan and Shafir, 2013.

16 Vergauwe, J., Wille, B., Feys, M., De Fruyt, F., & Anseel, F. (2015). Fear of being exposed: the trait-relatedness of the impostor phenomenon and its relevance in the work context. *Journal of Business and Psychology*, *30*(3), 565–581.

17 De Bruyckere, P. & Kirschne, P.A. (2016). Authentic teachers: student criteria for perceiving authenticity in teachers. *Cogent Education*, *3*(1), https://doi.org/1080/2331186X.2016.1247609.

18 Kennedy, J. (1995). De-biasing the curse of knowledge in audit judgment. *Accounting Review*, 249–273.

19 Camerer, C., Loewenstein, G., & Weber, M. (1989). The curse of knowledge in economic settings: an experimental analysis'. *Journal of Political Economy*, *97*(5), 1232–1254.

20 Reynolds, D., Sammons, P., De Fraine, B., Van Damme, J., Townsend, T., Teddlie, C., & Stringfield, S. (2014). Educational effectiveness research (EER): a state-of-the-art review. *School Effectiveness and School Improvement*, *25*(2), 197–230.

21 Askew, M., Rhodes, V., Brown, M., William, D., & Johnson, D. (1994). Effective teachers of numeracy. *Report of a study carried out for the Teacher Training Agency*. London: King's College London, School of Education.
Wray, D., & Medwell, J. (2001). *What Can Teachers of Literacy Learn from a Study of Effective Teachers?* Paper presented at the 12th European Reading Conference, Dublin, Ireland, 1–4 July. Retrieved from http://files.eric.ed.gov/fulltext/ED454500.pdf

4

MAKE THEM THINK!

This chapter will explore the following questions:

- What is the link between thinking and learning?
- How can you make everyone in the class think?
- When is thinking less good for learning?

On 22 March 2015, the psychologist Richard Wiseman wrote the following on Twitter:

> I keep seeing articles on enhancing student learning with tech etc. In my experience you just need to focus on 3 words – work really hard.[1]

The man has a point. A very good point, in fact. A point I would rather have made myself. After all, this is what we all want. A pill to learn a language. Learning in our sleep by listening to recordings. Each new 'trick' is enough to raise people's hopes and often enough to make them pay lots of money, in most cases unnecessarily.

Do you know what the most important 'trick' is for learning? It is called 'thinking' and, sadly, it works according to a very simple but inconvenient rule: the more you think, the more you learn. A pedagogue might reply to this: you can only learn properly through a meaningful experience, followed by a meaningful reaction. You need to notice something and process something if you want to save something in your long-term memory. But perhaps that is too abstract a concept to get by your working memory.[2] So let's begin this chapter with another exercise.

Here are four questions. Start by answering the first question, but cover all the other information with a sheet of paper. Then move on to the second question, still keeping the remaining information covered. Move on to the third question, with the same routine. Note down nothing while you are completing these first three tasks.

1. Set an X alongside the words that begin with a capital letter:

   Apple   shoe   Water   house   tree

2. Set an X alongside the things you personally own:

   Garden   bicycle   oil   gas fire   lemon

3. Set an X alongside the words that rhyme with fair:

   door   hair   fire   drink   stair

4. Note down as many words as you can remember from the three previous series (max. 15).[3]

Source: reprinted with kind permission from Dr. Hugo Schouppe

From which series could you remember the most? There is a good chance that it was the second series. You might think that this has something to do with what we learnt in Chapter 2. Perhaps you know things better that you own. Having said that, all the things in all three series are familiar to everyone. The real difference is that with the second series you need to think more than with series one and three. When marking the words with a capital letter, you only need to focus on the shape of the first letter of each word. Perhaps you scored a little bit better with the third series, because you needed to look at more of each word to reach the right answer. But it is only in the second series that you actually need to think about the whole word and what it means. Do you have a garden or not? Do you have a bicycle or not? And what about oil, a gas fire and a lemon?

The fact that you need to think more deeply about the second series explains why the majority of people remember the words in this series better than in the other two series. This exercise is based on the work of Craik and Lockhart, who developed the 'levels of processing' model. The basic idea is simple: the more deeply information is processed in the memory, the longer the memory trace in the brain will remain.[4] There has been a degree of criticism of this model, largely because Craik and Lockhart simply identified a phenomenon that exists, rather than explaining that phenomenon.[5] But that does not make the identification any less important.

Do you always have to think to learn?

Do you recognize the following text?

Najeneun ttasaroun inganjeogin yeoja

Keopi hanjanui yeoyureul aneun pumgyeok inneun yeoja

ami omyeon simjangi tteugeowojineun yeoja

eureon banjeon inneun yeoja[6]

Probably not, unless you are fluent in Korean. But what if I add the following phrase from the same song?:

Eh, sexy lady

For some of you a bell should now be ringing and the majority will know which song it is if I further add the words:

Op, op, op, op

Oppa....

Two words were still missing from this last piece of text, but I am sure that nearly all of you filled them in for yourself: Gangnam Style. This song by Psy was a worldwide hit in 2012. Of course, you have never been to school to learn this song by heart. Even so, you still recognized it. Most of you will have just picked it up, more or less passively. This is called latent learning. Some die-hard fans may have learnt the text consciously, but in most cases this will come from hearing it time after time after time.[7]

Is it then possible to learn everything passively, through constant repetition and exposure? Of course, the answer is no. That would be too easy. To understand this, we need to look at the distinction between primary and secondary learning made by Geary.

Primary learning processes relate to the learning of the mother tongue, learning to work together and learning to solve simple problems. These are things that children by and large are able simply to pick up, and we are often amazed at the way they do it. They learn by exploration and by imitation. In fact, it almost seems as if they learn by themselves, without much input from adults.

Secondary learning processes relate to things that cannot be picked up in this seemingly easy manner, but require considerable effort to acquire. This is often referred to as cultural knowledge and includes reading, writing, adding and subtraction, world knowledge, literature, new languages, and mathematics. It is no coincidence that these are the things often learnt at school.

Geary argues that primary learning processes are particularly important because they give us the means to deal with the secondary learning processes. At the same time, it would be wrong to think that a child can learn everything they need to learn on the basis of those primary processes.[8] This would be like expecting every child to understand gravity simply because an apple falls on their head. For things of this kind, it is better for a teacher to assist the child to learn by asking relevant questions. Or to put it another way: by making the child think.

FURTHER THINKING: WHY FLUORESCENT PENS DON'T WORK

In 2013, five cognitive psychologists under the leadership of John Dunlosky[9] published a comparative study of the effectiveness of different study methods. Have a look at what they found:

- What hardly works or not at all?
    - underlining or marking (according to some studies this can even work negatively)
    - re-reading
    - making summaries with full sentences (less negative than underlining, but still of limited effectiveness)
- What works well?
    - 'practice testing', making and doing small tests, not for points, but simply as a means to recall the study material (index cards and fiches can also be useful)

What is the difference between what works and what doesn't? When making and doing the small tests, the pupils really need to think. This is not necessarily the case with underlining, marking and re-reading.

In fact, marking can lead to another problem. Have you ever come across the following? You are sitting in an exam, you read the question, and you know where the answer is among all the mass of material you learned. You know what is above it and you know what is below it. But there is one thing you no longer know: the *%!# answer itself! So what is going on? Research by Sparrow et al.[10] has clearly shown what happens: with marking, you park your knowledge, but all you remember is where you parked it, not what you parked.

Using your brain optimally

Have you ever had the feeling that your brain is full? You are listening to a fascinating speech, but you suddenly notice that you have had enough and just switch off. Or you are studying and you know that a few minutes ago you knew almost everything, but now your eyes glaze over and you can hardly remember a thing. Or you want to concentrate, but there is so much noise around you that you can't focus.

These situations can be explained by what is known as cognitive load theory. This theory was developed in the 1980s by John Sweller, but actually dates back to the work of G.A. Miller in the 1950s. Miller argued that the capacity of our working memory is fairly limited. Sweller and his colleagues investigated how pupils and students attempt to solve problems. We will be looking at this theory in more detail in the final chapter of the book.

Make everyone think

In 2010, I first learned about Dylan Wiliam via the BBC documentary *The Classroom Experiment*.[11] In his scientific work on formative assessment[12] and in the approach he showed during the documentary, he combines various methods that centre around the importance of making pupils and students think or, rather, making sure that they *all* keep on thinking.

For example, Wiliam says that teachers should not ask children to put their hands in the air if they know the answer to a question. In this way, only about a quarter of the class are actually thinking. For this reason, it is much better to work with random choice; for example, by pulling names out of a box. But be careful: introducing this system can sometimes be frustrating for all concerned, and particularly for the stronger pupils who are used to answering a lot of questions or, as William puts it, 'dominating the conversation'. A next step might be to let all the pupils answer using small writing pads or boards that they all show to the teacher at the same time. This means that the less confident or less able pupils aren't able to switch off, while the stronger pupils continue to be constantly engaged and therefore become less frustrated.

Various other similar approaches are also possible, but they must all answer this question: how can I stimulate my pupils to think to the greatest possible extent?

A problem as the starting-point for learning

If we want to help children and young people to learn, might it not be a good idea to challenge them with a problem that needs solving? Surely that would make them think? The answer is a cautious 'yes', but with a number of 'buts'.

A first but...

In thinking about the use of problems in education, the literature usually makes a distinction between problem-based learning and problem solving. The difference has been clearly explained by Barrett:

> One of the most important points about problems in problem-based learning is that it is not a question that first the students receive inputs of knowledge (e.g. lectures, practicals, handouts, etc.) and then 'apply' this knowledge to a problem they are presented with later in the learning process. This type of a situation is not problem-based learning; it is problem solving (Savin-Baden 2000). It is like making a cake when you have already been given the recipe and all the ingredients. One of the defining characteristics of the use in problem-based learning is that students are deliberately presented with the problem at the start

of the learning process. This is like getting the challenge of preparing a celebratory meal for a special occasion where no recipes or ingredients are given.[13]

This distinction is important, because the learning effect of both methods can vary enormously for the learning of new content. It is the difference between the development of prior knowledge (problem solving) and the complete disregard of prior knowledge (problem-based learning). You can easily guess which is least suited: problem-based learning scores very poorly for the acquisition of new knowledge. Once the knowledge is present and you can use that knowledge to develop skills, problem-based learning becomes more effective.[14]

With problem solving, you also take a problem as your starting point, but then search together, teacher and pupils, to see how the problem can best be dealt with. You teach children, as it were, solving techniques, which they can later apply in other circumstances. This is a much more effective method, however there is a second 'but'...

A second but...

Your problem is not necessarily a problem for your pupils. I can still remember one of the first lessons I ever gave. It was a history lesson about classical antiquity and I said to my pupils that I often wondered whether the Romans also used to wear jeans. My plan was to use this interesting conjecture as a starting point for a lesson about Roman habits and customs, but this brilliant idea was shot to pieces within five seconds by one of the pupils who answered: 'Who cares?'

A good problem definition therefore requires the problem to be seen as a problem by those being taught. The problem needs to intrigue or must trigger a short circuit in the minds of your listeners. This can begin with phrases like 'it's not possible' or 'I don't understand'. Introductions like 'I think it's completely different' can also be effective. Research by Derek Muller has shown that learning outcomes are better if you take as your starting point misconceptions held by the pupils that can be corrected.[15] Of course, this comes at a price: the pupils often don't enjoy it as much. This is logical: it is harder work and it involves harder thinking. In short, it is learning.

A final but...

It is important that the problem is appropriate to, and connects with, the stage of the learning process in which the pupils and students currently find themselves. As mentioned in the previous chapter, you don't want to make things too hard, but you don't want to make them too easy, either. Assessing the right level of challenge is, er, challenging.

The limitations of thinking

Thinking is not learning

The difference between problem-based learning and problem solving makes clear that it is not possible to speak of in-depth learning simply because the pupils have been made to think long and hard.[16] It is perfectly possible that pupils think a great deal during the free solution of challenging problems in problem-based learning, but that they actually learn very little or even the wrong things.[17] If we want to achieve lasting learning outcomes, we need to stimulate pupils to relevant thinking, which focuses first and foremost on the development of prior knowledge and during which pupil misconceptions can be dealt with and corrected.

Enough is enough

Even with the most motivated, cleverest and happiest pupils and students, learning can grind to a halt if the circumstances are not optimal. Hattie and Yates speak of information overload, which is similar to the cognitive overload theory of Sweller. Whatever we call it, when does learning stop?[18]

- **If the lessons are too difficult or if you have too little prior knowledge.** We have already seen how important prior knowledge can be for effective learning. If everything is Chinese (assuming you don't speak Chinese), you will soon feel out of your depth and give up.
- **If you can't deal with stress.** If you are stressed and don't know how to deal with this awkward feeling, you will soon reach the point of overload.

- **If learning expectations are unrealistic.** Excessively high objectives and expectations for yourself and other will result in negative experiences during the teaching/learning process, which will again result in rapid overload and, ironically enough, reduced levels of effective learning.
- **If the teaching instruction and learning materials are poor.** Good lessons with clear and concrete examples are the best way to help pupils learn. If lessons and teaching aids are poor, the likelihood of overload increases.
- **If learning conditions are poor.** If there are too many distractions (your neighbour's laptop) or too much noise (the renovation works in the empty classroom next door), pupils will learn less and reach the point of overload more quickly.
- **If there is fear of evaluation.** Tests and other forms of evaluation can cause stress and anxiety, which are not conducive to good learning. This kind of stress can only be reduced if evaluation is as transparent, reliable and objective as possible.

To cut it short

- The likelihood is greater that you will learn something better and remember it longer if you are required to think a lot during the learning process.
- There is a difference between primary and secondary learning. The former is spontaneous; the latter isn't – it takes effort.
- Thinking is not necessarily the same as learning, certainly not if you think too deeply about the wrong things.
- Thinking learning needs the right conditions.

Notes

1 https://twitter.com/RichardWiseman/status/579583432231153664
2 See the exercise we did with the Wason test.
3 I found this exercise via http://www.vangorcum.nl/algemenepsychologie/geheugen/levels_processing.swf. This is no longer online.
4 Craik, F.I.M., & Lockhart, R.S. (1972). Levels of processing: a framework for memory research. *Journal of Verbal Learning and Verbal Behavior*, *11*, 671–684.

5   Eysenck, & Keane, M.T. (1990). *Cognitive psychology: A student's hand-book*, Lawrence Erlbaum Associates Ltd., Hove, UK.

6   www.azlyrics.com/lyrics/psy/gangnamstyle.html

7   The next chapter will look at the importance of repetition.

8   Geary, D.C. (2007). *Educating the evolved mind: reflections and refinements. Educating the evolved mind: Conceptual foundations for an evolutionary educational psychology*, 177–203.

9   Dunlosky, J., Rawson, K.A., Marsh, E.J., Nathan, M.J., & Willingham, D.T. (2013). Improving students' learning with effective learning techniques: promising directions from cognitive and educational psychology. *Psychological Science in the Public Interest, 14*(1), 4–58.

10 Check out: Sparrow, Liu, & Wegner, 2011 (Sparrow, B., Liu, J., & Wenger, D.M. (2011). Google effects on memory: cognitive consequences of having information at our fingertips. *Science, 333*, 776–778), but also: Storm, & Stone, 2015 (Storm, B.C., & Stone, S.M. (2015). Saving-enhanced memory: the benefits of saving on the learning and remembering of new information. *Psychological Science, 26*(2), 182–188). These studies deal with the way we delegate certain memory tasks to technology. If we know where we can find the knowledge, we don't need to remember it.

11 BBC (2010). *The Classroom Experiment*. London: BBC.

12 Wiliam, D. (2011). *Embedded formative assessment*. Bloomington, IN: Solution Tree Press.

13 Barrett, T. (2005). 'What is problem-based learning?' in G. O'Neill, S. Moore, & B. McMullin (Eds), *Emerging issues in the practice of university learning and teaching*. Dublin: All Ireland Society for Higher Education (AISHE).

14 This is evident in the work of (amongst others) Hattie (2009), but a recent comparative meta-meta-analysis reached exactly the same conclusion: see Schneider, M., & Preckel, F. (2017). Variables associated with achievement in higher education: a systematic review of meta-analyses. *Psychological Bulletin, 143*(6), 565–600.

15 Muller, D.A. (2008). *Designing effective multimedia for physics education* (Doctoral dissertation, University of Sydney, Australia).

16 Kirschner, P.A., Sweller, J., & Clark, R.E. (2006). Why minimal guidance during instruction does not work: an analysis of the failure of constructivist, discovery, problem-based, experiential, and inquiry-based teaching. *Educational Psychologist, 41*(2), 75–86.

17 The learning of incorrect material explains in part the negative score for problem-based learning in the meta-meta-analysis by Schneider & Preckel (2017).

18 See Hattie and Yates, 2013.

5

REPEAT, PAUSE, REPEAT, LINGER, PAUSE, REPEAT

This chapter will explore the following questions:

- Why is forgetting important for learning?
- Why is it better to use spaced repetition over time?
- What can go wrong if you use spaced repetition?

Have you ever worked deep into the night, revising for an exam? If so, you probably had good reason. After all, there are so many more other interesting things to do than revise, so I understand. But how much of what you learned could you still remember three days later? It is likely that you will be unable to recall a considerable amount.

What this proves is something that has already been known for quite some time. Since 1885, in fact.[1] It was then that Hermann Ebbinghaus conducted a number of experiments with his own memory. He tried to learn a list of pseudo-words, sounds and words that had no meaning, so that it was not possible to make any link with other things that he already knew.[2] Ebbinghaus discovered that initially it is possible to reproduce almost completely the things that you have learnt, but that the longer you wait to check what you still know, the less you will actually be able to remember.

This experiment resulted in the Ebbinghaus forgetting curve, a simplified form of which can be found in Figure 5.1.

Of course, it was initially open to question how much reliance could be placed on an experiment involving just a single test subject, who also happened to be the researcher himself. However, it soon

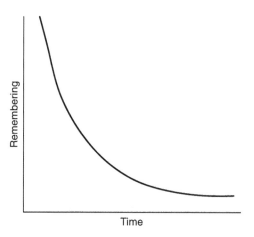

Figure 5.1 A simplified form of the Ebbinghaus forgetting curve

became apparent that Ebbinghaus's technique was easy to replicate, so that the experiment was repeated many times by others with similar results.[3]

Knowing how we forget the things we have learnt seems a banal subject for study, but Ebbinghaus's research led to some interesting follow-up work. Using the forgetting curve, it was subsequently discovered that repeating the learnt material with increasingly longer pauses is a powerful mechanism for the long-term memorization of content.[4]. What's more, content that has been learnt, forgotten and then learned again becomes more quickly and more firmly re-established in the memory. In other words, forgetting is crucial for learning.[5]

Remembering something very well and forgetting it completely are the two extremities of the same spectrum. How 'memorable' something is can, according to Bjork and Bjork,[6] be viewed in two different ways. In their theory of memory, now known as the New Theory of Disuse, they distinguish between what they call 'storage strength' (the extent to which something was remembered) and 'retrieval strength' (the extent to which something learnt can easily be recalled, or not).

When you were a teenager, you will no doubt have stored the telephone numbers of your best friends firmly in your memory (high storage strength). But you may have trouble remembering them, now that you have reached the age of forty (low retrieval strength).

Tests in school are actually practical exercises in retrieval strength: the extent to which pupils can quickly recall something they have learnt. It is more difficult to measure storage strength, although it is assumed that this will gradually increase, because we keep on learning more and more.

This theory is useful for explaining a phenomenon that you may well have come across with your own pupils and students. They have recently learnt something and can recall it quickly, if you ask them a question in class. At that moment, they have high retrieval strength. But that does not mean that they will continue to remember it in the long term, because we do not know to what extent they have high storage strength. However, you can give this storage strength a helping hand through spaced repetition.

How can you use spaced repetition in lessons?

Spaced repetition is often viewed, first and foremost, as a study method, but it is also an important insight with valuable classroom uses. In particular, it is crucial to return at regular intervals to things that have been previously learnt.

If you are mischievously inclined, you could regard a lesson series as a sequence of things to be forgotten. You have a first lesson, which according to the forgetting curve is soon forgotten, followed by a second lesson, which is equally soon forgotten, followed by a third lesson, etc., etc. Of course, no teacher worth his or her salt wants to look at his or her lessons in this way. It is therefore a good idea to build moments of repetition into your lesson series. This should not be a single repetition lesson halfway through or at the end in a series, but a systematic part of each individual lesson.

In concrete terms, your lesson series might look something like this:

- Lesson 1
- Lesson 2 with partial repetition of lesson 1
- Lesson 3 with partial repetition of lessons 1 and 2
- Lesson 4 with partial repetition of lessons 1, 2 and 3

The amount of repetition for the 'oldest' lessons decreases as the series progresses. A visualization of the difference between giving 'ordinary' lessons and lessons with spaced repetition, according to Lindsey and his colleagues, is given in Figure 5.2.

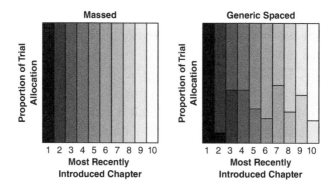

Figure 5.2   The difference between 'ordinary' lessons (left) and lessons with spaced repetition (right) (Lindsey, Shroyer, Pashler, & Mozer, 2014)

How can you integrate this easily into your lessons?

Building spaced repetition into your lessons doesn't need to be difficult. Price Kerfoot, a Harvard professor, has shown that something as simple as adding a few multiple choice questions to weekly emails to students can already have a positive effect. As a result, some of his students were required for a few minutes each week to answer questions in which new and older learning material was combined. At the end of the year, the students who had received the emails scored significantly better in their exams than the students who hadn't received the mails.[7]

Repetition by testing: the testing effect

Tests are often unpopular with teachers and pupils alike. The dreaded words 'Now take a sheet of paper...' have sent shivers down the spines of generations of school children. However, one of the best ways you can help your pupils to repeat what they have learned is by giving them regular short tests.[8] There are several advantages to doing this. It can increase the memory capacity for what was learnt, it slows down the rate of forgetting, it increases the chance of transferring insights to other domains, and enhances insights from own learning.[9] The positive learning effect of repeated testing was recently confirmed in a meta-analysis by Adesope and colleagues.[10]

FURTHER THINKING: HOW OLD IS THE
TESTING EFFECT?

When searching for the origins of the testing effect, reference is often made to the work of Gates in 1917.[11] However, the idea is much older. My good friend and mentor Paul Kirschner referred me to a much, much older source. As long ago as 1620, Sir Francis Bacon claimed: 'If you read a piece of text through 20 times, you will not learn it so easily by heart as if you read it ten times while attempting to recite it from time to time [i.e. testing yourself] and consulting the text when your memory fails'.[12]

Sadly, the testing effect will not work with every task you set your pupils. It only works if there is an average-to-good chance that the pupils will be able to remember the answers that appear in the test. If the test is so difficult that the pupils find it hard to remember both question and answer, or if the correct answer is not properly given by the teacher afterwards, the chance of effective learning is minimal.[13] Research also suggests that tests between learning moments have their strongest effect if the pupils do not simply look again at what they don't know, but if they look again at everything.[14]

FURTHER THINKING: REMEMBERING BETTER
WITH AMAZON?

One of the most fascinating research projects in 2014 combined the concept of spaced repetition with what we now call learning analytics, which is essentially the application of big data in education. This research by Lindsey and colleagues[15] attempted to assess which type of (repetition) questions are best asked to pupils over time. The team worked with a randomized controlled trial (RCT), with pupils who were divided randomly into three groups.

As a control, the first group were just given questions about the chapter they had seen that week (controlled). In other words, you could say that this group were given a succession of lessons based on the forgetting method. The second group were taught on the basis of the spaced repetition, with all the pupils being given the same repetition (massed spaced repetition).

(Continued)

The third group were given repetition on the basis of 'personalized review'. You can compare this with the systems used by online stores like Amazon: as soon as you have ordered something, you get a message saying 'people who bought this also bought that'. The message in personalized review translates into 'people who made this mistake often make these mistakes as well'. Figure 5.3 compares the different models.

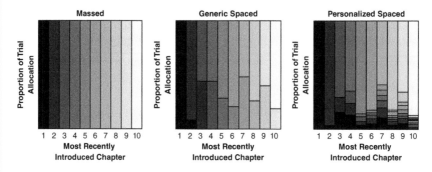

Figure 5.3 Ordinary lessons (left) versus massed spaced repetition (middle) versus personalized spaced repetition (right) (Lindsey, Shroyer, Pashler, & Mozer, 2014)

Let's take a more concrete look at personalized spaced repetition:

- Tom makes a mistake.

- Sarah makes the same mistake as Tom, but also a second mistake that Tom did not make. However, to make sure he doesn't do the same later on, this mistake is also included in Tom's repetition lessons.

- Ahmed makes neither the first nor the second mistake and so neither of them are included in his repetition lessons.

In other words, in the third group the pupils do not all get the same repetition lessons, but lessons that are personalized to reflect their previous test performances. This is an example of highly intense study differentiation. The actual lessons were given in the same way to all three groups, so that the researchers could better assess the impact of the three different repetition approaches.

What did the results show? In the exams covering the full course, the pupils with personalized spaced repetition lessons score on average 16.5% better than the control 'succession of forgetting' group, and 10% better than the more standard massed spaced repetition group. It was also shown that the personalized approach was most effective for the very first chapters that had been taught at the beginning of the course, months before the exam.

How can you use spaced repetition as a pupil or student?

Spaced repetition is one of the best methods of self-learning.[16] The most important concrete tips are:

- Start planning for your tests early enough and use a little bit of time each day: five hours spread over two weeks is better than five hours in a single session.
- Repeat the material learned in each lesson, but not immediately after that lesson.
- After you have repeated the learning content of the most recent lesson, also look at the most important content of previous lessons, to keep this fresh in your memory.[17]

This method also has consequences for the teachers and the school:

- Make and communicate your planning for tests well in advance.
- Give the pupils space and time for the necessary repetition.
- Set a good example and explain why the method works so well.

Spaced repetition as a method of study often involves the use of flash-cards. The cards can be written digitally or manually and consist of a question, or concept, and the answer, or a description, of the concept on the other side.

FURTHER THINKING: HOW LONG SHOULD YOU STUDY?

Pupils and students can sometimes quickly get bogged down because they don't really know how long they should study before they should move on to a new subject or take a break. It is, of course, difficult to set an exact time. Rohrer and Pashler summarize it as follows: a study session must be long enough so that you have a good grasp of the essentials, but not longer, because this then becomes a waste of time.[18] This can be a frustrating answer for people who were hoping to be given guidance in terms of hours and minutes! The problem is, however, that the time needed for effective study can vary depending on the complexity of the subject and the level of concentration of the pupil. In particular, this latter factor can vary dramatically, not only from person to person but also from moment to moment.

What are the possible problems with spaced repetition?

Under the motto 'nothing works in every case' and 'even the best medicines have side-effects', you need to be aware of the following potential pitfalls with shared repetition.

More repetition?

For some pupils – and, let's be honest, for some teachers as well – repetition is seen as being boring and unnecessary. Many methods make use of the insights relating to spaced repetition, but when faced with a shortage of time, it is easy for teachers to 'skip' the repetition session. In this way, you can transmit more learning material to the pupils in lesson sessions, but whether they actually learn it as well is another matter.

Repetition without thinking is pointless

In the previous chapter we underlined the importance of thinking. This continues to be important during repetition. Asking a pupil simply to re-read a text without thinking about the content has little value. Nor does just running through your own notes, without stopping to question and encourage thought.

FURTHER THINKING: DON'T LET YOURSELF BE (MIS)LED BY REPETITION

'I already know that.' You look at your notes and you recognize everything you see. 'So what should I be repeating?' I can hear you ask. You need to realize that recognizing learned material is much easier than reconstructing it from nothing in a test or exam. So it is no surprise that you can recognize lots of things when you just read through your notes. This relates to what we discussed earlier about the difference between the storage strength and retrieval strength of our memory.

To avoid this pitfall, there are other effective study methods that focus on *retrieval practice*, the active recovery of knowledge from the memory. In concrete terms, this means that it is useful from time to time to ask your pupils to put away their books and write down on a blank sheet of paper everything they can remember about the material they have learnt. This is an exercise that needs to be done with care and (again) thought. Afterwards, the pupils need to check how accurate and complete their recollections are, so that they know where to focus future repetitions. By using this exercise in the classroom, you can also encourage your pupils to use the same technique beneficially in self-study.

Facts are easier to repeat than insights

It is no coincidence that spaced repetition is popular for learning things like vocabulary lists with flashcards, with the foreign word on one side and the native language translation on the other. The same technique also works well for definitions. In his original research, Ebbinghaus used comparable words without meaning, words that he could not remember by linking them to something already concrete in his memory. You can still use spaced repetition to learn insights and applications, but you will need more and different exercises.

You remember the first thing better than the last thing

We have already suggested this in passing earlier in the chapter and it is a phenomenon that has appeared regularly in research relating to spaced repetition: it is generally easier to remember the first elements of what you learned than the last elements.[19] This is not illogical. In practice, the first elements are the ones that you will have repeated and tested most often. As a teacher, this is something that you need to bear in mind, so that you can put the most important insights first in your lessons.

Details can be lost

A 2014 study by Zachariah Reagh and Michael Yassa[20] has confirmed that spaced repetition works for the major points of content. However, they also concluded that this can sometimes have a negative effect on the memorization of details. The researchers suggest that the constant repetition of details results in them becoming more and more subsumed into other, large matters that are already known, so that they lose their distinctiveness.[21]

Learning mistakes from mistakes in a test

It is obviously no teacher's intention to teach pupils mistakes. Even so, many teachers still continue to consciously include mistakes in their tests. Multiple choice questions ask pupils to select the right answer from four options. This means that the pupil is 'forced' to read three wrong answers. Some experts argue that there is such a thing as *negative suggestion effect*.[22] Although research into the phenomenon is limited, the studies that do exist, according to Roediger and Karpicke,[23] consistently show that the effect can influence pupils who repeatedly see incorrect solutions in 'true-or-false' type questions. Having said that, the most recent meta-study[24] into the testing effect confirms the general effectiveness of spaced repetition based on multiple choice questions.

To cut it short

- Forgetting is important for remembering.
- Regularly repeat what has been learnt.
- Make the pauses between repetition moments gradually longer and longer.
- Regular short tests can stimulate learning.

Notes

1 Ebbinghaus, H. (1885). *Über das Gedächtnis. Untersuchungen zur experimentellen Psychologie*. Leipzig: Verlag von Duncker & Humblot.
2 A remarkable effort by Ebbingaus, if you remember what we said in Chapter 2.
3 Including, more recently, Murre, J.M., & Dros, J. (2015). Replication and analysis of Ebbinghaus' forgetting curve. *PLoS One, 10*(7), e0120644.
4 Including, in the 1930s, the research carried out by Spitzer, H.F. (1939). Studies in retention. *Journal of Educational Psychology, 30,* 641–657. Today, this is often associated with the work of Melton, Leitner and others.
5 Hattie & Yates, 2013.
6 Bjork, R.A., & Bjork, E.L. (1992). A new theory of disuse and an old theory of stimulus fluctuation. In A. Healy, S. Kosslyn, & R. Shiffrin (Eds),

From learning processes to cognitive processes: Essays in honor of William K. Estes (Vol. 2, pp. 35–67). Hillsdale, NJ: Erlbaum.

7 Kerfoot, B.P., DeWolf, W.C., Masser, B.A., Church, P.A., & Federman, D.D. (2007). Spaced education improves the retention of clinical knowledge by medical students: a randomised controlled trial. *Medical Education*, *41*(1), 23–31.

8 Benjamin, A.S., & Pashler, H. (2015). The value of standardized testing: a perspective from cognitive psychology. *Policy Insights from the Behavioral and Brain Sciences*, *2*(1), 13–23. But also see: Carpenter, S.K. (2012). Testing enhances the transfer of learning. *Current Directions in Psychological Science*, *21*(5), 279–283; Karpicke, J.D., & Grimaldi, P.J. (2012). Retrieval-based learning: a perspective for enhancing meaningful learning. *Educational Psychology Review*, *24*, 401–418; Roediger, H.L. & Butler, A.C. (2011). The critical role of retrieval practice in long-term retention. *Trends in Cognitive Sciences*, *15*(1), 20–27.

9 Kang, S.H. (2016). Spaced repetition promotes efficient and effective learning: policy implications for instruction. *Policy Insights from the Behavioral and Brain Sciences*, *3*(1), 12–19.

10 Adesope, O.O., Trevisan, D.A., & Sundararajan, N. (2017). Rethinking the use of tests: a meta-analysis of practice testing. *Review of Educational Research*, 0034654316689306.

11 Gates, A.I. (1917). Recitation as a factor in memorizing. *Archives of Psychology*, *6*(40).

12 Bacon, F. (2000). *Novum organum* (L. Jardine & M. Silverthorne, Trans.). Cambridge, UK: Cambridge University Press. (Original work published in 1620.)

13 Bjork & Bjork, 1992.

14 See, amongst others, Roediger III, H.L., & Karpicke, J.D. (2006). The power of testing memory: basic research and implications for education practice. *Perspectives on Psychological Science*, *1*(3), 181–210.

15 Lindsey, R.V., Shroyer, J.D., Pashler, H., & Mozer, M.C. (2014). Improving students' long-term knowledge retention through personalized review. *Psychological Science*, *25*(3), 639–647.

16 Dunlosky et al., 2013.

17 The Learning Scientists have made a very clear poster to explain this, which is now available in different languages. Check: www.learning scientists.org/

18 Rohrer, D., & Pashler, H. (2007). Increasing retention without increasing study time. *Current Directions in Psychological Science*, *16*(4), 183–186.

19 See, amongst others, Tulving, E., & Arbuckle, T.Y. (1963). Sources of intratrial interference in immediate recall of paired associates. *Journal of Verbal Learning and Verbal Behavior*, *1*(5), 321–334.

20 Reagh, Z.M., & Yassa, M.A. (2014). Repetition strengthens target recognition but impairs similar lure discrimination: evidence for trace competition. *Learning & Memory, 21*(7), 342–346.

21 Yassa, M.A., & Reagh, Z.M. (2013). Competitive trace theory: a role for the hippocampus in contextual interference during retrieval. *Frontiers in Behavioral Neuroscience, 7,* 107.

22 Remmers, H.H., & Remmers, E.M. (1926). The negative suggestion effect on true–false examination questions. *Journal of Educational Psychology, 17,* 52–56.

23 Roediger & Karpicke, 2006.

24 Adesope et al., 2017.

6

THE IMPORTANCE OF PRACTICE

This chapter will explore the following questions:

- Why do we still need to practise or even drill pupils at school?
- How do you evolve from a beginner to an expert?
- Why at the same time is practice alone not enough?

Help, I'm standing in front of a door!

Imagine that every time you find yourself standing in front of a door you need to ask yourself how a door works. Imagine that every time it takes you ten minutes to rediscover that you need to push that handle thing downwards and then another ten minutes to find out whether you need to push or pull the door before it opens. Let's be honest: it would make life pretty difficult!

Or imagine that a footballer would need to think how to kick the ball every time a member of his team passes the ball to him. Or that a guitarist would need to think in the same way about the next chord of the song he is playing. It is probably true that at some point in their life both footballer and guitarist had to think a lot more carefully about these things, so that everything went a lot slower, but in the meantime they have both 'automated' their different ways of playing.[1]

I gave these examples to one of my sons, when he was fed up with learning his multiplication tables by heart. The reasoning is, of course, the same: if you need to make a conscious calculation every time someone asks you 'how many is nine times eight?', you will end up losing an awful lot of time. The more you are able to make your knowledge of multiplication tables automatic, the more mental bandwidth you make free to think about other things; for example, more complex calculations. Yes, I know: drilling exercises – or perhaps better automation exercises – are not popular. They never have been and they never will be. There is nothing creative about them and they cost a lot of time and effort. But automation is crucial if we want to create the room to be creative and complete the next steps in the learning process with less hard work.

Learning to read is also a form of automation. Once again, imagine if it was necessary every time you see a group of letters together on a page that you need to consciously think about which words those letters might be capable of forming. It would take you quite a while to read your way through this book, which contains over 40,000 of those letter groups, separated by spaces.[2]

But be careful: like most things, automation also has its limitations. Once something is automated, you might find you have a tendency to more easily overlook mistakes. If you see a group of letters that you automaticaly recognize as a word, you might forget to notice that there is a mistake in the spelling of that word ('automatically' has two l's). According to Schneider, Dumais and Shiffrin, automation of mental processes allows you to work more efficiently (in terms of time) but less flexibly with the automated material itself.[3]

FURTHER THINKING: THE IMPORTANCE OF EARLY AUTOMATION FOR FURTHER LEARNING IN OTHER SUBJECTS

We are doing a lot of imagining in this chapter. So imagine now that reading is not automatic. This means that reading a text – any text – will take a lot more time. You can compare it with the reading of this sentence (which I have deliberately made a bit more difficult: my apologies):

J bn tp ibqqz uibu zpv ibwf nbef uif fggpsu up efdjqifs uijt tfoufodf, cfdbvtf ju tipxt uibu zpv bsf sfbmmz joufsftufe jo kfbsojoh. Ps uibu zbv bsf tjnqmz dvsjpvt cz obuvsf.

The text is written in a code, in which each letter has been changed to the next letter in the alphabet: A becomes B, B becomes C, etc., until Z becomes A. So the message actually reads:

I am so happy that you have made the effort to decipher this sentence, because it shows that you are really interested in learning. Or that you are simply curious by nature.

Of course, you cannot fail to have noticed that this makes the reading of the sentence unnecessarily complex, so that you are more concerned with the actual deciphering of the letters than with the content of the message. So just think what it must be like for a child who cannot read well who is asked by his teacher to read out a text in a history lesson...

What repetition is for the remembering of knowledge, practice is for the improvement of skills. But to go from good to excellent takes more than just occasional practice: it takes deliberate and sustained practice.

Deliberate practice

Deliberate practice is associated primarily with the work of Anders Ericsson, who recently summarized his thirty years of research with Robert Pool in the book *Peak*.[4] According to Ericsson, the book describes how ordinary people are capable of performing remarkable things.

FURTHER THINKING: NATURE OR NURTURE

One of the most noticeable things in the work and thought of Ericsson is that he adopts a fairly extreme 'nurture' standpoint. In other words, he believes that just about everything is learnable. Anyone can learn to play the piano, everyone can run a marathon, and so on. This is diametrically opposed to the 'nature' vision, which argues that many skills are predetermined, often genetically. There is, of course, something to be said for this point of view. In his standard work *The Blank Slate*, Steven Pinker[5] deploys a huge arsenal of examples of abilities and talents that seem to be inborn rather than inbred. Ericsson concedes

(Continued)

that a person's natural predisposition can play a role, but he minimizes the extent of that role. For example, he accepts that tall people will generally find it easier to play basketball well. However, his extreme nurture perspective is no longer widely shared.[6]

The nature–nurture debate is a long-standing one and points of view are seldom as extreme as Ericsson's. Most experts see a complex interaction between both elements. A study in 2013 attempted to quantify to what extent differences in school results could be attributed to natural aptitude. To make this possible, the results of 11,000 twins in the United Kingdom were compared.[7] The conclusion was that 58% of the differences in the core tests could be explained by personal aptitude. That is a high figure, but the research does not conclude that this aptitude is necessarily fixed from birth. For mathematics and scientific thinking – which are apparently the disciplines most susceptible to influence by nature – there were still 42% of other influences at play. Moreover, the influence of aptitude is only greater in optimal circumstances. Where children grow up in less favourable circumstances, the influence of the environment plays a proportionally bigger role.[8]

Ericsson has described the criteria that deliberate practice must satisfy:

- *Deliberate practice develops skills that others already possess and for which effective training techniques exist.*

  The most remarkable aspect of this first criterion is that Ericsson states that the practice programme must be drawn up by a teacher or coach who knows how the skill can best be developed. In other words, the pupil or student cannot do it alone.

- *Deliberate practice takes place outside the trainee's comfort zone and demands constant effort to try to perform marginally above their current level of performance.*

  You probably recognize this. This takes us back to Vygotsky's zone of proximal development. Ericsson admits that this is probably not much fun. If you are training for a sport and you see someone ahead of you suffering badly, you know that this is precisely what awaits you every time you go out to practise! On the other hand, reaching a goal you knew would be difficult can be highly satisfying, because of the experience of success it brings.

- *Deliberate practice is based on clearly defined objectives and is concerned with improving a certain aspect of the desired performance and not just with a vague general improvement.*

This coincides with matters we discussed earlier, such as scaffolding. These clear objectives are essential for the following criterion, which is:

- *Deliberate practice is precisely what the name implies: it is deliberately focused on specific goals and targets; this means that every practice session demands the learner's full attention and conscious effort.*

This almost sounds like playing with words, but it nonetheless connects with the importance of thinking that we mentioned earlier. Simply following instructions is not enough to achieve the desired effect. The learner must be fully conscious of the objectives at all times and must be able to assess whether they have been successfully attained. In consultation with the teacher-trainer, corrections can be made to the objectives and the practice, as and when necessary. This brings us to the following criterion:

- *Comments on, or adjustments to, the practice as a result of those comments are a fundamental characteristic of deliberate practice.*

Here Ericsson is describing, almost in passing, what I regard as one of the most fundamental, although often overlooked, of all didactic principles: the principle of gradualness, specifically focused here on self-direction. In a teaching process designed to take the learner from the status of a beginner to the status of an expert, passing through all the different steps in between, it is important in the early phase that the teacher gives frequent comments and feedback, but it is equally important that the learner gradually takes control of the learning process. Learning to recognize and correct your own faults is a vital step in the learning process.

- *Deliberate practice leads to the development of effective mental representations and subsequently becomes dependent on those representations.*

In order to control and correct yourself, you first need to have a good mental picture – a mental representation – of the way things should be. Imagine that you want to learn how to dance the tango. It is crucial to know what this dance looks like when it is performed perfectly, so that you can identify where your version of the dance is currently less than perfect and can adjust those elements accordingly. As the learner, the image in your head is the reference by which you can monitor and control your learning. These mental representations develop gradually during the learning and practice processes, and are, in turn, critical for achieving further self-directed development.

- *Deliberate practice nearly always involves the acquisition of new skills or the correction of previously acquired skills through the improvement of a number of its specific aspects.*

  With this last criterion, Ericsson concludes that teachers must teach clear basic skills to beginners.

Running through all these different criteria, one of the most noticeable features is the way that deliberate practice runs parallel with many of the different subjects we have already touched upon in this book. Ericsson underlines the importance of strong guidance and direct, albeit differentiated, instruction for the acquisition of basic skills, in a manner not dissimilar to the processes for acquiring basic knowledge. It is also significant that he attaches similar importance to the figure of the teacher, mentor or (sports) coach.

Once you understand the concept and importance of mental representation, it is not difficult to understand why the role of the teacher is such an important one, certainly during the initial phase of a learning process. A beginner seldom has a clear picture in his or her mind of where they want to go, of the way things should be. You need mental representations to control and improve your own performance. In the absence of these representations, self-direction becomes impossible.

A beginner will also find it difficult to assess what the next step or challenge should be. In fact, it is sometimes difficult for teachers to know how far their pupils have already come and whether or not they are ready to take the next step, with the necessary degree of concentration and effort.

Can you practise everything with this gold standard of deliberate practice?

According to Ericsson, no you can't. In his own research Ericsson focused primarily on excellent performance in, for example, sport. Perhaps for this reason, he believes that in most cases deliberate practice only works if it takes place in a context of competition: the learner must want to be the best at something.

A meta-analysis carried out under the leadership of Brooke Macnamara[9] attempted to chart the effect of deliberate practice in the different sectors where it is used. It was concluded that deliberate practice could account for 26% of the differences in playing chess, 21% of the differences in playing music and 18% of the differences in sports performance. This means that deliberate practice has a clear added value, but it is evident that other factors – such as natural aptitude – also play a role.

If we look at the results for education in the same meta-analysis, deliberate practice now accounts for just 4% of the differences, and in the work environment the impact is as little as 1%. However, we need to take account of the fact that nearly all the educational research included in Macnamara's analysis was focused on university students, which makes the results open to question when considering the applicability to learning in school. This applies equally to the working environment, where the total number of studies was very limited.

If we look more closely at other aspects of research in the educational field, it seems reasonable to conclude that the effect of deliberate practice within education has the potential to be significant, depending on the specific area of study. A further meta-analysis looking at the use of deliberate practice during the training of doctors concluded that there is a clear, large and positive effect.[10]

FURTHER THINKING: IS DELIBERATE PRACTICE BEST DONE ALONE OR IN A GROUP?

Macnamara also investigated the difference in effect between deliberate practice conducted with individual guidance and in groups. The differences that the researchers were able to identify were not sufficient to say that the individual approach gives a significant added value.

Is practice enough?

Let me be clear on this point: no! There are two reasons why 'just' practising is not enough:

- Automation, as discussed at the start of this chapter, is something you must do so that you can follow the steps in the learning process. It relates to certain skills that can be rightly described as basic or fundamental; from cutting techniques for people working in the coconut industry to the recognition of opening moves for world class chess players. This definition of 'basic' varies not only from one field of expertise to the next, but also in relation to the phase of the learning process in which the learner finds themselves. Which leads us on to the second reason, namely...

- Continually repeating the same practice exercises seems to have little or no effect, no matter how often or how long you do them.[11] The essential element in deliberate practice is a learning pathway that encourages the learner to constantly set new boundaries. If you practise the same guitar chord for 10,000 hours, you will perhaps know everything there is to know about it, but you still won't be able to play a song, because you only know a single chord.

Finally, it is necessary to remember that repeated practising and drilling are not always experienced as something pleasant by those who are required to do so. If education consisted solely of practice of this kind, not only would we lose our pupils, but it is also seriously open to question whether we would actually teach them enough. This is yet another argument in favour of using a varied selection of teaching and learning methods.

To cut it short

- The automation of certain skills is crucial for matters such as counting and reading.
- Automation is the result of a great deal of practice, but to achieve excellence takes much more.
- To become very good at something, deliberate practice can make the difference, based on a clear plan to set new personal boundaries in a succession of prearranged steps.
- A learner must be able to make mental representations of the objectives towards which they are working, so that it is possible to identify and correct their own errors.

Notes

1 See, amongst others: Logan, G.D. (1988). Toward an instance theory of automatization. *Psychological Review*, *95*(4), 492; Neves, D.M., & Anderson, J.R. (1981). Knowledge compilation: mechanisms for the automatization of cognitive skills. *Cognitive Skills and their Acquisition*, 57–84. Hillsdale, N.J.: Erlbaum.

2 Abadzi, H. (2008). Efficient learning for the poor: new insights into literacy acquisition for children. *International Review of Education*, *54*(5–6), 581–604.

3 Schneider, W., Dumais, S.T., & Shiffrin, R.M. (1984). Automatic and control processing and attention. In R. Parasuraman & R. Davies (Eds), *Varieties of attention* (pp. 1–27). New York: Academic Press.

4 Ericsson & Pool, 2016.

5 Pinker, S. (2003). *The blank slate: The modern denial of human nature*. Penguin.

6 See also: Hambrick, D.Z., Oswald, F.L., Altmann, E.M., Meinz, E.J., Gobet, F., & Campitelli, G. (2014). Deliberate practice: is that all it takes to become and expert? *Intelligence*, *45*, 34–45; Macnamara, B.N., Hambrick, D.Z., & Oswald, F.L. (2014). Deliberate practice and performance in music, games, sports, education, and professions: a meta-analysis. *Psychological Science*, *25*, 1608–1618; Macnamara, B.N., Moreau, D., & Hambrick, D.Z. (2016). The relationship between deliberate practice and performance in sports: a meta-analysis. *Perspectives on Psychological Science*, *113*, 333–350.

7 Shakeshaft, N.G. et al (2013). Strong genetic influence on a UK nationwide test of educational achievement at the end of compulsory education at age 16. *PLoS One*, *8*(12), e80341.

8 Turkheimer, E., Haley, A., Waldron, M., D'Onofrio, & Gottesman, I.I. (2003). Socioeconomic status modifies heritability of IQ in young children. *Psychological Science*, *14*(6), 623–628.

9 Macnamara et al., 2016.

10 McGaghie, W.C., Issenberg, S.B., Cohen, M.E.R., Barsuk, J.H., & Wayne, D.B. (2011). Does simulation-based medical education with deliberate practice yield better results than traditional clinical education? A meta-analytic comparative review of the evidence. *Academic Medicine: Journal of the Association of American Medical Colleges*, *86*(6), 706.

11 Porter, G.E., & Trifts, J.W. (2014). The career paths of mutual fund managers: the role of merit. *Financial Analysts Journal*, *70*(4), 55–71.

7

METACOGNITION: TEACHING YOUR PUPILS AND STUDENTS HOW TO LEARN

This chapter will explore the following questions:

- What is metacognition and why is it important?
- How can you work at metacognition with your pupils?
- How should you not work at metacognition?

Sigh

Every time I start talking about 'leaning to learn' in one of my lessons, you can almost hear my students' sighs and groans echo around the room. If I ask them why, they all point back to metacognition lessons they had at school. Lessons of which, it seems, the large majority do not have fond memories!

Even so, when Daniel Muijs[1] announced at researchED Amsterdam what he saw as the five certainties to emerge from educational effectiveness research, there was one of the five that at the same time was both crystal clear and slightly confusing: the importance of working on the metacognition of your pupils and students. This was, of course, the purpose of the lessons that had left such a bad taste in the mouths of so many of my students. So what's the problem?

Why is the importance of metacognition crystal clear? The more pupils know about the best way to learn, the better they will be able to do it and the more they will ultimately learn. According to research by

John Hattie, the learning of metacognitive strategies has an effect size (d) of 0.69. So why at the same time is this also slightly confusing? Because people often don't know what metacognition is, how to deal with it and how to work with it effectively. So perhaps my students are right. But then so are John Hattie and Daniel Muijs. See? I said it was confusing!

What is metacognition?

Let us begin with the first challenge: defining what metacognition is and is not. Cognition relates to our thinking, but what does it mean if you put a 'meta' in front of it? Metalanguage is a language that you use to talk about language; for example, about the grammatical structure of a language. You would also use metalanguage to explain about spelling rules. In short, a metalanguage consists of words to help you talk about words.

There is also such a thing as metahumour. Metahumour is when you joke about making jokes. In concrete terms, this might go something like: 'An Englishman, an Irishman and a Scotsman are sitting in a bar. And the barman says: "Is this a joke, or what?"'. So as you might expect, metacognition is cognition about cognition; or to put it more simply: thinking about your own thinking, as Flavell[2] described it in 1979. For this reason, metacognition is sometimes also known as higher order thinking.

Zimmerman[3] distinguishes two elements in metacognition: awareness of your own thinking and knowledge of your own thinking. Veenman[4] also makes a distinction between two different elements: on the one hand, knowledge about your own cognitive system – this is the same as Zimmerman – and, on the other hand, control over that cognitive system. This is different from Zimmerman's awareness and already starts to make things more complicated.

As if this were not enough, the grandfather of metacognitive studies John Flavell[5] also made a double distinction; in his case, between metacognitive knowledge and metacognitive experiences. A metacognitive experience is when you are aware of your own actions. For example, you might suddenly realize that your approach to something is wrong or come to the insight that you do not have enough information or knowledge to complete a task properly.

So now we already have three duos to describe metacognition and there are plenty of others circulating in academic circles as well. But it all remains frustratingly abstract. Fortunately, we can also approach metacognition in another, more practical manner. If there are so many indications that metacognition can result in a positive learning effect, why don't we just look at the things that are measured to reach this conclusion? Today's most widely used, and most empirically grounded, distinction is similar to the three already mentioned above, but (as you might expect) not precisely the same: it is the distinction between metacognitive knowledge and metacognitive skills.

According to Schraw and his colleagues,[6] metacognition consists of the following three elements:

1. Descriptive knowledge: knowledge about yourself as the learner and about the factors that influence your learning performance;
2. Procedural knowledge: knowledge of different strategies and approaches;
3. Conditional knowledge: knowledge about when, where and why you should use a particular learning strategy or approach.

Consequently, metacognitive skills relate to three main activities: planning, monitoring and evaluating. Planning is about the setting of clear objectives, the activation of prior knowledge (see Chapter 2), the selection of the correct learning strategy, and the choice of the best sources and aids. Monitoring is about testing yourself as the learner, to see if you are actually learning. And evaluating is about looking at what you have learned and assessing whether or not it is enough.

FURTHER THINKING: WHO ACTUALLY DIRECTS LEARNING?

Metacognition is often mentioned in the same breath as self-regulation and self-direction. The Education Endowment Foundation also links these two concepts in their toolkit:

(Continued)

Self-regulation refers to managing one's own motivation towards learning as well as the more cognitive aspects of thinking and reasoning. Overall these strategies involve being aware of one's strengths and weaknesses as a learner, such as by developing self-assessment skills, and being able to set and monitor goals. They also include having a repertoire of strategies to choose from or switch to during learning activities.

In other words, the ultimate objective is to help pupils take learning into their own hands. Vermunt[7] has reflected on the question of who actually directs learning, who ensures that something is learnt. He identified three different types of directive impulses in pupils and students:

1. **Internal direction or self-direction:** these are the ultimate super-pupils and students, who learn spontaneously and independently; and if they can, they will sometimes even learn more than they need to learn, purely out of interest!

2. **External direction:** these pupils and students learn because somebody tells them they must. If there were no teachers, parents or textbooks the likelihood that they would ever learn anything at all is pretty small, and they would certainly never do more than the absolute minimum necessary.

3. **Directionless strategy:** These pupils and students do not learn by themselves or from their environment; they find it difficult to learn and don't approach the task in the right way (for example, constantly repeating things in the hope that something might eventually stick).

But to be honest, this categorization is much too strict.[8] In reality, every pupil and student is self-directing to some degree. Just look at the definition for the directionless strategy: even there the child takes the initiative to repeat what he or she is supposed to have learnt, which is clearly a form of internal direction. It is just the approach that is wrong.

For whom is metacognition important?

Put simply: everyone. And the importance of metacognition – and, by extension, self-direction – increases as the child gets older. It is also important to know that in most children a basic form of metacognition develops spontaneously by looking at and copying their peers, their parents, their teachers, and so on, although this is often neither sufficient nor effective. Moreover, research has shown that the spontaneous learning of metacognition from role models in the child's environment can result in significant differences; for example, between children with different socio-economic statuses.[9] Together with intelligence, metacognition has a significant impact on learning and academic success, but metacognition is *not* a synonym for intelligence.[10]

Perhaps you can recognize the following description in one of your pupils or maybe even in your own child. The pupil is bright, so bright that they hardly need to study in primary school. They simply remember everything taught in the lessons. This even works for a time in secondary school and possibly even in further education, until a moment arrives when this automatic approach is no longer enough and the pupil finally needs to study. But they can't. Or they don't know how to. As a result, their grades begin to fall and keep on going downwards, notwithstanding the child's obvious intelligence. How can this happen? It can happen because a child with a high level of intelligence does not necessarily have a high level of metacognition. In fact, there is a closer correlation between school success and metacognition than there is between school success and intelligence, something which led Muijs and his colleagues to conclude that metacognition can compensate for 'cognitive limitations', or, to put it another way, being less naturally smart.[11]

How can you best work at improving metacognition?

In recent years, a number of researchers have published meta-analyses about effective metacognitive strategies.[12] Hattie[13] summarizes these findings as follows: to work effectively with metacognition, you need to:

1. practise within the context of what needs to be learnt;
2. use tasks from the same domain as the subject(s) that are being dealt with;
3. ensure that enough is being learned;
4. make this sufficiently clear, so that pupils *know* that they are learning how to learn or are working at metacognition.

Within this process, the pupil or student needs to stop and reflect about the how, when, where and why of the different strategies that can be used when learning. In the course of this book, we have already mentioned several different effective study methods; for example, thinking up your own questions or making flashcards to test learnt material, as we discussed in Chapters 4 and 5.

But there are even more effective strategies that pupils and students can learn *within* the context of your subject. Based on the different meta-analyses, it is possible to rank these strategies in accordance with the three metacognitive skills we discussed earlier:

1. Planning your own learning.

    a. Set clear objectives: what are the priorities and what is secondary?
    b. Set a fixed order for everything you need to do and a fixed time by when you have to do it.
    c. Set rewards and punishments for your successes and failures in relation to your set objectives; for example, no television tonight if you haven't learnt the first 10 pages of your course.

2. Monitoring your own learning.

    a. First decide the way you want to learn things:

        i   Mnemonics, as a means to memorize certain rules; for example, the rhyme 'I before E except after C' to remember the spelling of words like 'believe' and 'receive' or 'Please Excuse My Dear Aunt Sally' to learn the order of maths operations (Parentheses, Exponents, Multiply, Divide, Add, and Subtract)
        ii Learning things by heart through (spaced) repetition, if necessary.

    b. Put into your own words the steps you need to take to complete a task successfully; for example, naming the different steps you need to take to solve a problem.
    c. Make notes during the lesson, revise them afterwards and re-read them together with any texts and tests as preparation for the following lesson or test.

3. Evaluating your own learning.

    a. Set the standards you need to meet.
    b. Ask for help from other pupils, teachers or anyone else if there is something you don't understand or if you have not been able to do something.

There are other metacognitive strategies and study methods, such as visualization, which will be discussed in a later chapter.

Is working at metacognition the same for every subject and learners of every age?

Two meta-analyses by Dignath and Büttner[14] have made clear that the effect of working at metacognition can indeed vary, depending on subject and age. The authors made two separate analyses: one for primary education and one for secondary education. They concluded that there were positive effects for both age groups, but that there were a number of nuances that teachers need to take into account (see Table 7.1).

Table 7.1   Metacognition at primary and secondary school (based on data from Dignath & Büttner, 2008)

	Primary school	Secondary school
Similarities		
Who gives the training?	For both age groups: lessons given by the researchers had more effect than lessons given by teachers.	
How long and how often should you work at metacognition?	For both age groups: the greater the number of training sessions, the greater the effect.	
Differences		
Focus on?	The training must work at motivation and the encouragement of pupils.	The training must work at expanding the repertoire of strategies.
Group work when training for metacognition	Negative effect; the pupils work better individually at improving their metacognitive skills	Positive effect; the pupils work better in groups at improving their metacognitive skills.

It is crucial that enough opportunities to practise are given to pupils and students, irrespective of their age. The sufficient practising of different strategies is also, so that their use becomes second nature, in keeping with what we discussed in Chapter 6. This 'automation' increases the likelihood that the metacognitive skills will not only be used in the subject in which they were first learned. The analyses also revealed that working at metacognition can have different levels of effect in different study areas. In general – and irrespective of pupil age – working to improve the metacognitive effect seems to work better in mathematics lessons than in language lessons or other subjects. But this does not mean that you should not work at metacognition in languages and other lessons. Quite the reverse!

FURTHER THINKING: EXECUTIVE FUNCTIONS

Intelligence and metacognitive skills are today frequently mentioned in conjunction with a third element: executive functions. These are the higher cognitive processes that are necessary to be able to learn and work. Like metacognitive skills, there are different gradations of executive functions, such as resisting sudden impulses, being able to plan, being flexible, being able to concentrate, and so on. At the moment, there seems little doubt that these functions play a significant role in learning.

So why have I not devoted a separate chapter to these functions? I have not done so, because although there is enough evidence to show that they are crucial for learning, it is less clear if they are something we can actually work at improving. There are various studies that show a positive impact, but a recent large-scale meta-analysis of the past twenty-five years of research found little to suggest a genuine long-term positive effect.[15] Of course, this is a relatively new field in educational enquiry, so at this stage I would not want to label it as a myth (as I have done in the past for many other educational fairy tales). However, it seems to me that it is still too early to include a chapter on executive functions in a book about educational approaches whose certainty is not in doubt.

How you should *not* work at metacognition

My groaning and sighing students at the start of the chapter were probably right: it is better not to give separate lessons about metacognition, because in general they are not very effective.[16] Metacognition is so interwoven into the very act of learning that it is difficult to see it in isolation from the subject matter being taught. We have already seen earlier in the book that transfer from one domain to another is one of the biggest challenges in education. For this reason, metacognition is best approached as part of the learning of general skills.

That being said, an idea has been circulating for the past forty years that writing might be a way to work at the improvement of metacognition. However, a meta-analysis by Bangert-Drowns, Hurley and Wilkinson[17] makes clear that while writing in general may have a small positive effect on learning, long and specific writing exercises result in almost no benefit. Using writing as an aid to learning in secondary school also has no positive effect.

To cut it short

- Working to improve metacognitive knowledge and skills can be very effective.
- Work on metacognition in all subjects and not as part of a separate subject.
- The learning of metacognition skills varies depending on pupil age and therefore requires different approaches for primary and secondary schools.

Notes

1 Muijs, 2016.
2 Flavell, J.H. (1979). Metacognition and cognitive monitoring: a new area of cognitive-developmental inquiry. *American Psychologist, 34*, 906–911.
3 Zimmerman, B.J. (2002). Becoming a Self-Regulated Learner: an overview. *Theory into Practice, 41*(2), 64–70.
4 Veenman, M.V.J. (2013). Training metacognitive skills in students with availability and production deficiencies. In H. Bembenutty, T. Cleary, & A. Kitsantas (Eds), *Applications of Self-Regulated Learning across diverse disciplines: A tribute to Barry J. Zimmerman* (pp. 299–324). Charlotte, NC: Information Age Publishing.
5 Flavell, J.H. (1985). *Cognitive development* (2nd edn). Englewood Cliffs, NJ: Prentice Hall.
6 Schraw, G., Crippen, K.J., & Hartley, K. (2006). Promoting self-regulation in science education: Metacognition as part of a broader perspective on learning. *Research in Science Education, 36*, 111–139.

7 Vermunt, J.D.H.M. (1992). *Leerstijlen en sturen van leerprocessen in het hoger onderwijs. Naar procesgerichte instructie in zelfstandig denken.* Amsterdam: Swets & Zeitlinger.

8 Vermunt, J.D.H.M. (1998). Onderwijskundig Lexicon, Deel III. Leeractiviteiten van leerlingen. L. Verschaffel & J.D.H.M. Vermunt (Red.), *Het leren van leerlingen*, 29846. Alphen Aan De Rijn: Samson.

9 Leutwyler, B. (2009). Metacognitive learning strategies: differential development patterns in high school. *Metacognition and Learning, 4,* 111–123.

10 See amongst others: Veenman, M.V.J., Wilhelm, P., & Beishuizen, J.J. (2004). The relation between intellectual and metacognitive skills from a developmental perspective. *Learning and Instruction, 14,* 89–109; Veenman, M.V.J., & Spaans, M.A. (2005). Relation between intellectual and metacognitive skills: age and task differences. *Learning and Individual Differences, 15,* 159–176.

11 Muijs, D., Kyriakides, L., van der Werf, G., Creemers, B., Timperley, H., & Earl, L. (2014). State of the art – teacher effectiveness and professional learning. *School Effectiveness and School Improvement, 25*(2), 231–256.

12 See amongst others: Hattie, J., Biggs, J., & Purdie, N. (1996). Effects of learning skills interventions on student learning: a meta-analysis. *Review of Educational Research, 66*(2), 99–136; Dignath, C., & Büttner, G. (2008). Components of fostering self-regulated learning among students: a meta-analysis on intervention studies at primary and secondary school-level. *Metacognition and Learning, 3*(3), 231–264; Lavery, L. (2008). *Self-regulated learning for academic success: An evaluation of instructional techniques* (Doctoral dissertation). Auckland: ResearchSpace.

13 Hattie, 2012.

14 Dignath, & Büttner, 2008.

15 Jacob, R., & Parkinson, J. (2015). The potential for school-based interventions that target executive function to improve academic achievement: a review. *Review of Educational Research, 85*(4), 512–552.

16 Hattie et al., 1996.

17 Bangert-Drowns, R.L., Hurley, M.M., & Wilkinson, B. (2004). The effects of school-based writing-to-learn interventions on academic achievement: a meta-analysis. *Review of Educational Research, 74*(1), 29–58.

8

EVALUATE AND GIVE FEEDBACK

This chapter will explore the following questions:

- What is formative evaluation and why is it so important?
- What is feedback and why is it so important?
- How do you give effective feedback?
- When can things go wrong with feedback?

- How can a pupil or student know if their knowledge is correct?
- How can a pupil or student know if they are repeating enough?
- How can a pupil or student know if they are practising enough?
- How can a pupil or student know what the next step in their practice or learning path should be?

The answer to all these questions is feedback as part of formative evaluation. According to Black and Wiliam (amongst others), this is the only way to improve educational performance.[1] Feedback is the information that pupils and students get in response to their level of performance in relation to a set objective. This information can come from a parent, a teacher, or even a fellow pupil or student.

Different forms of evaluation

Feedback is often linked to the principle of formative evaluation. To understand properly what formative evaluation is all about, it is first necessary to make a distinction between product and process evaluation on the one hand and summative and formative evaluation on the other hand.

Product and process evaluation are essentially a matter of 'what' you are evaluating. Product evaluation checks whether you have reached a pre-set objective. Process evaluation examines how you reached that objective.

Let's make this more concrete. If the objective is 'draw a tree', product evaluation will decide whether or not the child has indeed been able to draw a tree. Process evaluation will look at how the child drew the tree: not only the method of drawing, but also, for example, how long the child took, did they start straight away, were they distracted, and so forth. Process evaluation can also be about your way of working as a teacher. For example, did you explain the task properly, did you use the right examples, did you give the child enough time to complete the task?

Formative and summative evaluation are less about the 'what' and more about the 'why'. Summative evaluation is evaluation that assesses or passes judgement. Is the child ready to move forward to the next year? Should he or she be allowed to change subjects? Summative evaluation therefore comes after the completion of something (a module, a course, a year). Formative evaluation is evaluation that gives guidance to the learner *during* the learning process.

These different types of evaluation are summarized in Figure 8.1.

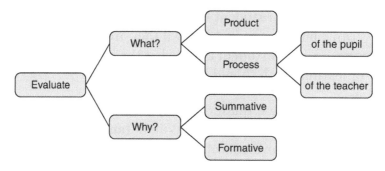

Figure 8.1 Types of evaluation

Confusion can arise if people see 'product' and 'summative' as synonyms, or regard 'process' as being the same as 'formative'. This is a mistake. There are four possible combinations.[2]

Let's explore an example of this in the classroom. Imagine that the task is 'draw an angle of 90 degrees'.

Formative process evaluation:

> The teacher checks to see how pupil A has drawn the right angle and gives feedback on the method of working.

Formative product evaluation:

> The teacher looks at the right angle and gives feedback about the end result.

Summative process evaluation:

- The teacher checks to see how pupil A drew the right angle in the end of year exam and decides on that basis whether the pupil has passed or failed.
- The teacher checks to see how the class as a whole drew the right angle in the end of year exam and then decides whether he will teach this task in the same way during the next school year.

Summative product evaluation:

> The teacher looks at the right angle drawn by pupil A and awards points that will determine whether the pupil has passed or failed for mathematics.

Feedback given in formative evaluation can therefore relate to both process and product, and is intended to help the pupil or student during the learning process.

If you look back at the previous chapters, you will see that we have already looked at several examples in which formative evaluation played a crucial role. It is a part of direct instruction; it is an aspect of the personalized review approach; and in the chapter on the importance of practice, it was a key element in the concept of deliberate practice. Last but not least, the giving of feedback about the learning process is integral to any work to improve metacognition.

FURTHER THINKING: QUALITY CRITERIA FOR GOOD EVALUATION

In recent years many books have been written about evaluation and it is not the intention of this book to go too deeply into this subject. However, I do want to outline the main quality criteria for good evaluation:

1. **Validity:** are you actually measuring what you want to measure?

(Continued)

Some examples:

- A pupil is asked to study five chapters of a book but in a test only gets questions over the first two chapters. In that case, the *learning objective representivity* or *content validity* is compromised. The evaluation does not reflect the aims that were set.

- Imagine that you explain a particular concept in a lesson. In the test you do no more than ask the students to reproduce this insight correctly. But have you then measured this insight? There is a good chance that all the students will be able to do is repeat what they heard you say during the lesson, but you will not know whether they actually understand the insight. In this case, the *learning objectives validity* or *conceptual validity* is put at risk: you don't check to see that the objective has been reached to the required level.

- As already mentioned, the purpose of summative product evaluation is to assess whether the pupil or student is ready to move on to the next module, subject, year, etc. If the evaluation does not do this adequately, there will be a lack of *predictive validity*.

2. **Reliability:** to what extent are you measuring what you want to measure objectively?

    An assessor who is influenced by a pupil? A test where some students are more advantaged than others? A mistake that counts more heavily against pupil A than against pupil B? These are just some examples of inconsistencies that can harm objectivity or reliability. You can enhance reliability by agreeing clear assessment criteria in advance, for example, by having the same piece of work assessed by different teachers.

3. **Transparency:** does the student or pupil know how and on the basis of what objectives he or she will be evaluated?

4. **Workability or effectiveness:** Imagine that you want to set up a reliable evaluation process for teachers at a training college. How often do you need to observe the trainee teachers in action? Hill and colleagues[3] suggest a minimum of six lessons that are seen by five different assessors. However, this can be expensive and time-consuming, so it may not be workable in many situations.

Of course, you can look at other criteria or make alternative categorizations, but the above brief summary should at least make clear that you sometimes need to balance different considerations. Exams with multiple choice questions can be very efficient and reliable, but their validity can sometimes be open to question, because with this method you cannot measure everything and it is also easier to recognize knowledge than to reproduce it from scratch in an open question.[4]

The dream they call feedback

There was already considerable interest in feedback in education, but following the publication of John Hattie's *Visible Learning*[5] this interest has become even greater. Hattie claimed that the effect size for feedback was a spectacular 0.73, although a recent meta-analysis has suggested that on average it works better in higher education than in primary or secondary education.[6] Together with Helen Timperley,[7] Hattie had previously made two other much quoted meta-analyses specifically on this subject, which again revealed a large average effect.

But does this mean that feedback is the holy grail of learning? Let me put it another way. Does this mean that all forms of feedback are equally good? No, probably not. What's more, feedback alone can never replace education. It is simply not possible to see feedback as something separate from the entire learning process.[8]

Conditions for optimal feedback

Set clear objectives

How can you know if someone is doing well or badly without objectives? What are you going to compare them with? In the previous chapter about deliberate practice, I described how a learner must have a clear mental picture of what he or she is working towards. It is this mental picture that a teacher or mentor needs to try to encapsulate in learning objectives. It also explains why it is crucial to communicate these objectives clearly to the learner.

Make sure the learning is observable

How can you give feedback if you can't see whether or not someone has reached the set objective? It is for this reason that De Block and Heene underline the importance of concrete and observable lesson objectives.[9] These objectives – which you should note down before you start to prepare your lesson[10] – must be the yardstick you use to measure the pupils' performance and your feedback will deal with the extent to which they have achieved these objectives (or not) and how they can do better next time. It is not without good reason that John Hattie's different books often have variants of 'visible learning' in the title. In this way, he emphasizes the effect of being able to see what takes place in the classroom. This visibility is important for adjusting both the learning process of your pupils and students and your own education processes through feedback. The regular setting of tests (we discussed the testing effect in an earlier chapter) can also help your pupils and students to see how they are progressing and allows you as teacher to further guide them with feedback in the right direction.

Make objectives challenging but achievable

If the objectives you set the learner are unachievable, you can give as much feedback as you like but it won't make any difference: it will be of little or no benefit to your pupil or student. Conversely, if objectives are too easy or lacking in challenge, no feedback will be necessary. Too much or too little is never good for learning.

Give good teaching!

Feedback has no point if the pupil or student is being pointed in the wrong direction as a result of inadequate or incomplete teaching. To be told that you are performing poorly when in fact you were poorly or even incorrectly informed can only lead to frustration. If you see that the majority of your pupils are not reaching their objectives, perhaps you should be less concerned about giving feedback and more concerned about a different and better way of giving your lessons.

What is the best way to give feedback?

According to Hattie and Timperley,[11] effective feedback answers the following three questions:

1. Where am I heading? (which the authors refer to as 'feed up')

    Here you can see the link with objective-based learning: the learner needs to know what the objective is and what results must be achieved.

2. What have I done? (which they refer to as 'feed back')

    This relates to both the product, 'to what extent have I reached the set objectives?' – and the process – 'how did I approach those objectives?'

3. What is the next step? (which they refer to as 'feed forward').

How should the learner progress further? What can he or she do differently to reach the set objectives? What should be their next objective?

Kamphuis and Vernooj suggest that in this context there is a need to think about 'more challenge, higher expectations, more control over the learning process, learning how to better answer questions, etc.'[12]

It is not possible to view the above three questions in isolation. They belong together, because they all relate to the same objectives. You can use these three questions at four different levels:

1. Task level:
   - How well was the task understood?
   - How well was the task performed?
   - Was the objective reached?

2. Process level:
   - What process was used to carry out the task and how successful was it?

3. Metacognitive level:
   - To what extent could the pupil or student monitor and adjust their approach to the task?

4. Personal level:
   - This involves making comments about the pupil or student as an individual, such as 'You're a good learner!'

Several experts, including Hattie and Timperley, argue that for feedback to be effective it needs to be frequent, detailed and specific. They also contend that the first three levels are more effective than the fourth one. But if you are going to give someone praise, make sure you do it as specifically as possible: 'You're a good learner because...'

It is also important for its effectiveness that the giving of feedback should not be delayed for too long, but should follow the learning performance as soon as possible. According to a meta-analysis by Van der Kleij and colleagues delayed feedback has a clear negative effect.[13]

But there is one final but very important condition for successful feedback that is often overlooked: how the feedback is interpreted by the learner.[14] If the pupil or student does not accept or properly understand the feedback, it will be of little value.

Dylan Wiliam has summarized the possible reactions of pupils as shown in Table 8.1.

Table 8.1 Reactions to feedback (adapted from Wiliam, 2012)

Reaction of the pupil.	The feedback more or less says that...	
	the objectives were more than adequately reached.	the objectives were not adequately reached.
Changes behaviour.	the pupil will try less hard to do his/her best.	the pupil will try harder to do his/her best.
Changes objective.	the pupil will become more ambitious and want to achieve more.	the pupil becomes less ambitious.
Loses heart and abandons the objective.	the pupil finds the objective too easy.	the pupil finds the objective too difficult.
Does not accept the feedback.	the pupil ignores the feedback.	the pupil ignores the feedback.

This summary prompted David Didau to warn against too frequent feedback, citing Soderstorm and Bjork[15] to support his argument. And it is true that there are only two pupil reactions in the above schedule that are positive for learning:

- The pupil will become more ambitious and want to achieve more.
- The pupil will try harder to do their best.

This seems to me to be a recommendation not only to look at the learning process, but also to follow up on how the pupil deals with the feedback by monitoring their reactions and taking corrective action, where necessary. In this sense, the pupil's ability to deal with feedback is a good way to decide how often you should give it.

According to Kamphuis and Vernooy[16], it is important to answer the following questions if you want to give effective feedback:

- What am I going to tell the pupil or student about their work?
- How am I going to get this message across?
- What will the pupil or student do with this message?
- How will this improve their learning?

When is feedback not effective?

The simple answers are fairly obvious: feedback is not effective if it:

- is not specific
- is not frequent enough
- is not detailed enough
- is delayed for too long
- encourages one of the six non-positive reactions in Dylan Wiliam's table.

Research by Carless[17] shows that in addition to non-specific and unclear feedback, difficult to understand feedback can also have a negative effect. Even more importantly, feedback that undermines the confidence of the pupil or student can lead to similar and potentially more undesirable negative effects. This point was, perhaps, best summarized by Hattie in 2003:[18] it is not about giving more feedback (which you might imagine, given the emphasis in the literature on 'frequent'), but about giving better and more qualitative feedback at the right moment for each individual pupil or student.

The questions that teachers can best ask, according to Kamphuis and Vernooy,[19] are therefore:

- How much feedback does a pupil get during an average day?
- How much feedback does a pupil at risk of underachieving get during an average day? Is it twice as much as an average pupil?
- Does the feedback help the pupil to make progress?
- Does the pupil think they are making progress?

FURTHER THINKING: GIVING MARKS?

This is a frequently discussed point: should teachers give their pupil 'marks out of ten'? When Dylan Wiliam scrapped the giving of marks during the BBC documentary *The Classroom Experiment*, many of the more able pupils reacted negatively. As they saw it, they no longer had the chance to distinguish themselves. In fact, some of them tried to work out their own approximate 'points score' on the basis of the number of positive or negative comments they received. Is this understandable? It is, to a degree. Points, marks and grades are the most rudimentary form of feedback. In one sense, a figure or letter can be experienced by pupils as something clear, but it says very little about which objectives the pupil has reached and which not. As a result, the pupil is unclear about what to do and where to go next.

Does this mean we should get rid of points altogether? To do so would be a learning process for teachers and pupils alike, not forgetting parents! If we are talking about summative evaluation, then in my opinion points certainly still have a role to play. But there is also one absolute taboo: never just give points without adding clarifying comments. This is always experienced negatively by pupils and explains why feedback is so important for learning.

Equally detrimental, and pointless (no pun intended), is the use of average or median scores in school reports. What are you comparing when you do this? You are no longer looking to see if the child reached the set objectives, but are only looking at how the child performed in relation to the other pupils who just happen to be in the same class. Tom is in class A and Mary is in class B. They both take the same test and they both score 7 out of 10. However, Tom is in a strong class, where the average or median score was 8 out of 10. As a result, he will probably be told that he needs to do better in future. In contrast, Mary is in a weaker class, where the average or median score is 6 out of 10. She will probably be congratulated on her performance, even though it was no better than Tom's!

A class average or median score is only relevant as part of the evaluation process of the teacher, not the pupils. If the class average or median is low, the teacher needs to think about changing their lesson content and methods

To cut it short

- Formative evaluation and feedback can be very effective, but not all feedback is effective.
- Feedback can only be effective if it is objective-based and if the teaching is good enough.
- Feedback is more effective if it is detailed and specific.

- The feedback must be frequent enough and must be given soon after the learning performance.
- It is important to monitor how the pupil reacts to feedback and what they do with it.

Notes

1 Black, P., & Wiliam, D. (2010). Inside the black box: raising standards through classroom assessment. *Phi Delta Kappan*, *92*(1), 81–90.

2 Castelijns, J., Segers, M., & Struyven, K. (2011). *Evalueren om te leren. Toetsen en beoordelen op school*. Coutinho: Bussum.

3 Hill, H.C., Charalambous, C.Y., & Kraft, M.A. (2012). When rater reliability is not enough: teacher observation systems and a case for the generalizability study. *Educational Researcher*, *41*(2), 56–64.

4 Hattie & Yates, 2013.

5 Hattie, 2009.

6 Van der Kleij, F.M., Feskens, R.C., & Eggen, T.J. (2015). Effects of feedback in a computer-based learning environment on students' learning outcomes: a meta-analysis. *Review of Educational Research*, *85*(4), 475–511.

7 Hattie, J., & Timperley, H. (2007). The power of feedback. *Review of Educational Research*, *77*(1), 81–112.

8 Kamphuis, E., & Vernooy, K. (2011). Feedback geven. Een sterke leerkrachtvaardigheid. *Basisschoolmanagement, jrg*, *25*, 4–9.

9 De Block, A., & Heene, J. (1993). *De school en haar doelstellingen*. Antwerpen: Standaard Educatieve Uitgeverij.

10 Dear teacher training student. I know that you note down your objectives at the end of your lesson preparation. My colleagues know that also. I hope that this book will make clear why this is wrong. Will it help? I don't know. But do you know what: give it a try?

11 Hattie & Timperley, 2007.

12 Kamphuis & Vernooy, 2011.

13 Van der Kleij, Feskens & Eggen, 2015.

14 See, amongst others: Hsieh, I.L.G., & O'Neill, H.F. (2002). Types of feedback in a computer-based collaborative problem-solving group task. *Computers in Human Behavior*, *18*, 699–715; Jaehnig, W., & Miller, M.L. (2007). Feedback types in programmed instruction: a systematic review. *The Psychological Record*, *57*, 219–232.

15 David Didau blogged on this subject on www.learningspy.co.uk/featured/getting-feedback-right/, referring to Soderstrom, N.C., & Bjork, R.A. (2015). Learning versus performance: an integrative review. *Perspectives on Psychological Science*, *10*(2), 176–199.

16 Kamphuis & Vernooy, 2011.
17 Carless, D. (2006). Differing perceptions in the feedback process. *Studies in Higher Education, 31*(2), 219–233.
18 Hattie, J. (2003). *Teachers make a difference: What is the research evidence?* Auckland: The University of Auckland.
19 Kamphuis & Vernooy, 2011.

9

USE MULTIMEDIA, BUT USE IT WISELY

This chapter will explore the following questions:

- When do you learn more using multimedia and when do you learn less?
- Which didactic principles apply to the use of multimedia?
- How can you learn better using images?

Do I need to draw you a picture?

Imagine that you meet an older couple who ask you for directions. You start to explain, but while you are going through the steps one by one, you notice that the couple are looking at you willingly but uncomprehendingly. Then you can hear yourself say: 'Do I need to draw you a picture?' To which the answer is probably: 'Yes'.

This simple sentence conceals one of the oldest didactic principles known to education: the presentation or visualization principle. In fact, we already discussed this principle in part in Chapter 2, where we learnt how important it is to bypass the spam filter of our working memory. In the meantime, we have also learnt how we can achieve this using the insights of cognitive psychological research: by using words and images together.

On the basis of a review of 11 studies, Mayer[1] showed that pupils who receive an explanation in both words and images remember more than pupils who are taught the same content using either just words or just images. For example, you cannot explain to pupils how

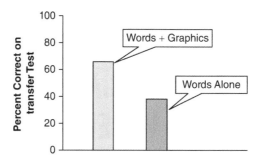

Figure 9.1 Learning is better from words plus graphics than from words alone (Clark & Mayer, 2016; adapted from Mayer, 2009)

a pump works unless you can make this visible. Words alone will not be enough.

Mayer summarized this neatly in a new didactic principle that relates closely to the visualization principle:

- The multimedia principle: text and image is better than text alone.

The basic idea underpinning this principle is that we have two channels in our head (which explains why it is sometimes called 'the dual channel theory'), one for words and another for images. Learning will take place optimally if both channels are addressed at the same time.

FURTHER THINKING: THE ORIGIN OF THE DUAL-CODING THEORY

This line of thought about multimedia is based on the so-called dual-coding theory developed by Allan Paivio in 1971.[2] Figure 9.2 makes clear what the link is between this theory and thinking about the spam filter we call our working memory (see Chapter 2).

The theory contends that if only words are used (spoken and/or written), then it is only possible to talk of one type of coding. If, however, you add images to the words, the coding in the brain takes place a second time: first visually and then verbally. In this way, the combination of words and images leaves a double trace in the brain, so that they are more easily and better remembered.

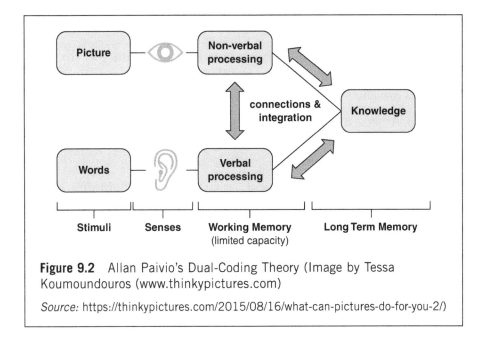

Figure 9.2 Allan Paivio's Dual-Coding Theory (Image by Tessa Koumoundouros (www.thinkypictures.com)

Source: https://thinkypictures.com/2015/08/16/what-can-pictures-do-for-you-2/)

Of course, it wouldn't be education if everything was as simple and straightforward as that! Amongst others, Sung and Mayer[3] have shown that this multimedia principle works, but that it suffers from a number of limitations. Firstly, it is important that the images are not simply added as 'decoration'. They must have an added value in terms of content. So yes, by all means combine words and images with each other, but don't just add photos or pictures you think are 'nice', but have little or nothing to do with the subject being taught. This, according to Mayer, leads on to another principle:

• The coherence principle: avoid unnecessary words, images and noises that are unrelated to the lesson content.

It is not so difficult to understand why this should be. If our working memory only has a limited capacity, it is important not to over-tax it with material that is unnecessary or irrelevant. This relates to another important aspect of the dual-channel theory in connection with multimedia learning; namely, that both channels in our head – the visual and the textual – also have a limited capacity. So you need to be careful not to overload these either!

To make this clear, consider the following example:

Imagine that you have a group of 200 pupils and you divide them randomly into two groups: Group A and Group B. Both groups are shown a video about storms.

Group A sees a video of storms, thunder and lightning, etc., accompanied by a voice-over that gives additional explanation about what is on the screen.

Group B sees the same video of storms, thunder and lightning, etc., accompanied by the same voice-over that gives additional explanation, but this time with extra subtitles in the same language.

Which group do you think will remember the most? Amongst others, Austin[4] has demonstrated that Group A will remember more than Group B. In my previous book about educational myths,[5] we discussed how you can't expect pupils to multitask. You can't read and listen at the same time. Or, if we follow the reasoning in Mayer's theory on multimedia learning, you cannot overload a channel and expect it to work. In this example, the word 'channel' had been overloaded by a double dose of words in spoken and written form.

Mayer summarizes this in yet another didactic principle:

- The redundancy principle: image and audio is better than image and audio plus text.[6]

In this example, there are two important aspects that you may not have noticed. The example was of a scientific-technical nature. As we shall see later in the chapter, this was no coincidence. The redundancy principle is more applicable to material of this kind than, for example, the learning of a language. The second aspect worthy of note is that the subtitles were in *the same language* as the voice-over.

FURTHER THINKING: DUAL CODING AS A STUDY METHOD

Pupils can use dual coding by themselves to improve their studying.[7] The most important concrete tips are:

- Find the images in your study material. Look at these and compare them with what is written.

- Look at the images again and explain their meaning in words.

- Visualize: try to make a visual representation in your head of the things you are trying to learn.

Should there be no text at all on the screen?

No, the above does not mean that there can no longer be any text whatsoever on your slides. There are some situations where text on slides can still give (limited) added value:

- If no images, animation, video, graphics, illustrations etc. are visible on the screen;[8]
- If the pace of the lesson is slow enough so that there is time to absorb all the information, both textual and visual;
- If some words are difficult to understand if they are only spoken.

More important still: offering just a limited number of key words can have added value. Yue, Bjork and Bjork[9] showed that adding shortened versions of what was said can have a positive learning effect. In this regard, it is crucial that what is spoken and what is written on the screen do not in any way contradict each other, and also that the tempo of the image medium is not too fast. The irony is that during this experiment by Yue and colleagues, in which students were shown a PowerPoint about the origins of a star, the students preferred to have the images with just the spoken commentary. Yet while their research confirmed the redundancy principle when a lot of text was used, the use of limited text was shown to have a clear added value, even though the students regarded this as a less positive experience.

What does this mean for practice?

Let's make these insights concrete with a number of examples. Figure 9.3 shows a slide that summarizes some of the key points on prior knowledge from Chapter 2 using the acronym 'APPLE'.

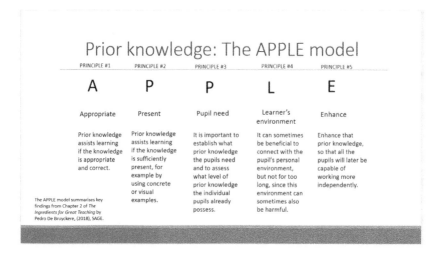

Figure 9.3 A slide with too much text

It is not a good idea to use this slide in a lesson; it is more an eye test than a learning tool!

You can always let your pupils and students just read such a slide, but as a teacher it is better to keep silent while they do – in the hope that they are indeed reading.

The following option (Figure 9.4) is a better version of the slide:

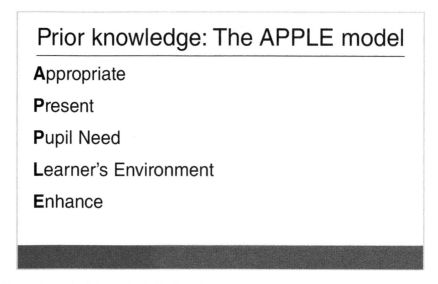

Figure 9.4 A slide with limited text

Perhaps it is also advisable to show each word separately. The following slide (Figure 9.5) is also an option:

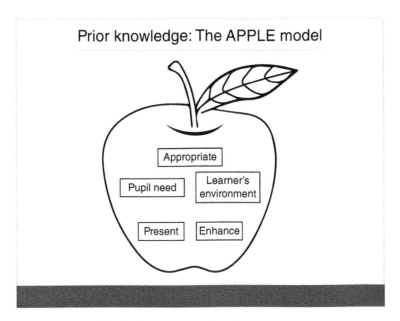

Prior knowledge: The APPLE model

Figure 9.5 A slide with limited text and an image

FURTHER THINKING: BUILD UP DIAGRAMS AND SCHEDULES TOGETHER WITH YOUR PUPILS

Imagine that you want to show your pupils in class a diagram, or schedule, that explains how the water cycle works. It is best to first show them the complete cycle and then explain the individual component parts one by one. Alternatively, you can build up the schedule or diagram one step at a time with your pupils. Research by Fiorella and Mayer[10] has shown that step-by-step information is easier to learn. And this does not mean that you need to do this *per se* with blackboard and chalk. In their research, Fiorella and Mayer used four different versions of videos about the Doppler effect. The pupils who were shown a video in which the information was presented step by step remembered the most.

Dual channel and learning languages

The combination of a letter and a word to help pupils learn to read is a theory much older than Mayer's multimedia principle. But what about learning foreign languages by using the dual channel theory?

For learning *in* a foreign language, in the first instance the same rules would apply. Research by Mayer, Lee and Peebles from 2014[11] revealed that the addition of moving images via videos helped pupils to better understand a language (thereby confirming the multimedia principle), although the addition of subtitles seemed to have no beneficial effect (thereby confirming the redundancy principle). But in this experiment the focus was on understanding learning material *in* a second language, not the learning *of* that language.

For the learning *of* a foreign language subtitles do seem to help, contrary to the redundancy principle. In an older research study dating from 1992, Martine Danan[12] compared three videos, one of which only contained the foreign language (French), while a second version had subtitles in the non-foreign language to match the spoken foreign language commentary. The third video was a little out of the ordinary: the dialogue was in the non-foreign language, with subtitles in the foreign language that the pupils were hoping to learn. Surprisingly enough, the results showed that this third version was best for learning vocabulary in the foreign language. But be careful: using these 'reversed subtitles' does not work well with young children.[13]

In short, videos in a foreign language with subtitles and a video in your own language can both help pupils to learn vocabulary in a foreign language. A video in your own language with subtitles in a foreign language can help even better, but only if the pupils are old enough. But can videos and subtitles also help to learn grammar? Research in Leuven by Lommel, Laenen and d'Ydewalle[14] shows that the results are generally disappointing. It seems that grammar is too complex to be 'deduced' spontaneously from the foreign language without the necessary instruction and explanation, which brings us back to the distinction between primary and secondary learning processes we discussed in Chapter 4.

FURTHER THINKING: A STUDY METHOD FROM CLASSICAL ANTIQUITY THAT STILL WORKS!

There is an ancient study method that still works, although it is perhaps nowadays more famous from the Sherlock Holmes television series: the memory palace, also known as the loci method. This method was first developed during classical antiquity, when it was used to learn long speeches and dissertations by heart in the days before using notes was acceptable. What does the method involve? You need a place that you know very well; your home, for example. The better you know the place, the better the method will work. You need to be able to visualize the place in your mind extremely well. Next, you link all the things you want to remember to specific features of your chosen location. A popular exercise with this technique is remembering the list of all the American presidents. You can see Lincoln sitting at your dining room table, Jefferson hanging up his hat in the hall, etc. Later on, you can recall the names from your memory simply by taking a mental walk through your memory palace.

This method involves different elements we have already seen. On the one hand, you link new content to things you already know very well, as we saw in Chapter 2. On the other hand, it is similar to the levels-of-processing exercise that we did at the start of Chapter 4. In addition, the visualization of the material to be learnt also ties in with the dual channel or dual coding theory we read about earlier in this chapter.

The method is very popular with the participants in memory competitions,[15] such as the remembering of random words or the memorization of the order of a shuffled pack of cards. In 2017, the record for the card test stood at a fantastic 493 cards in 10 minutes and 910 cards in half an hour. The world record for learning random words by heart is 318 words in 15 minutes.[16] It is also worth noting that these memory champions do not necessarily have a higher IQ than you and me.[17] This means that we can all learn and use this technique.

There is, however, one important reservation that needs to be mentioned: this method helps you to memorize things, but it doesn't help you to understand them. Using the memory palace, it is relatively easy to learn the first hundred figures after the decimal point of the number pi, but this does not mean that you know what this number represents or how you can use it to calculate the radius of a circle.

When does the dual channel theory not work?

It is thought that the effectiveness of the combination of image and word is linked to the presence or absence of prior knowledge. This means that beginners would have more need of the use of both channels, while pupils with plenty of prior knowledge of a subject would find little additional benefit. There are also some experts who think that the use of images in instances where there is plenty of prior knowledge can even hinder learning.[18]

To cut it short

Megan Smith and Yana Weinstein of the *Learning Scientists*[19] have summarized this theory in a number of practical tips:

- If you want to explain a diagram, do it verbally and not with text or more images.
- Present image and text at the same time, so that the pupils do not need to memorize one while trying to process the other.
- Avoid redundancy by avoiding the simultaneous use of the spoken dialogue and written text.
- Only use useful information. Using images and sounds 'for fun' can distract pupils and increase cognitive loading.

Notes

1 Mayer, R.E. (2009). *Multimedia learning* (2nd edn). New York: Cambridge University Press.
2 Paivio, A. (1971). Imagery and language. *Imagery: Current Cognitive Approaches*, 7–32. New York: Academic Press.
3 Sung, E., & Mayer, R.E. (2012). When graphics improve liking but not learning from online lessons. *Computers in Human Behavior*, 28(5), 1618–1625.
4 Austin, K.A. (2009). Multimedia learning: cognitive individual differences and display design techniques predict transfer learning with multimedia learning modules. *Computers & Education*, 53(4), 1339–1354. But also, for example, Jamet, E., & Le Bohec, O. (2007). The effect of redundant text in multimedia instruction. *Contemporary Educational Psychology*, 32(4), 588–598.
5 De Bruyckere, Kirschner & Hulshof, 2015.
6 Mayer has developed even more principles of multimedia learning. In this work I only focus on three of them, but the others are also well worth reading.
7 Mayer, R.E., & Anderson, R.B. (1992). The instructive animation: helping students build connections between words and pictures in multimedia learning. *Journal of Educational Psychology*, 4, 444–452.
8 Adesope, O.O., & Nesbit, J.C. (2012). Verbal redundancy in multimedia learning environments. *Journal of Educational Psychology*, 104(1), 250–263.
9 Yue, C.L., Bjork, E.L., & Bjork, R.A. (2013). Reducing verbal redundancy in multimedia learning: an undesired desirable difficulty? *Journal of Educational Psychology*, 105(2), 266.

10 Fiorella, L., & Mayer, R.E. (2016). Effects of observing the instructor draw diagrams on learning from multimedia messages. *Journal of Educational Psychology, 108*(4), 528–546.

11 Mayer, R.E., Lee, H., & Peebles, A. (2014). Multimedia learning in a second language: a cognitive load perspective. *Applied Cognitive Psychology, 28*(5), 653–660.

12 Danan, M. (1992). Reversed subtitling and dual coding theory: new directions for foreign language instruction. *Language Learning, 42*(4), 497–527.

13 See, amongst others: d'Ydewalle, G. & Pavakanun, U. (1995). Acquisition of a second/foreign language by viewing a television program. In P. Winterhoff-Spurk (Ed.), *Psychology of media in Europe: The state of the art – perspectives for the future* (pp. 51–64). Opladen, Germany: Westdeutscher Verlag GmbH; d'Ydewalle, G., & Van de Poel, M. (1999). Incidental foreign-language acquisition by children watching subtitled television programs. *Journal of Psycholinguistic Research, 28*, 227–244.

14 Lommel, S., Laenen, A., & d'Ydewalle, G. (2006). Foreign-grammar acquisition while watching subtitled television programmes. *British Journal of Educational Psychology, 76*(2), 243–258.

15 See, among others: Yates, F. (1966). *The Art of Memory*. London: Routledge & Kegan Paul; Foer, J. (2011). *Moonwalking with Einstein: The art and science of remembering everything*. London: Penguin.

16 Check the current world records on http://iam-stats.com/records.php

17 Conway, A.R.A. (2003). Working Memory Capacity and its relation to general intelligence. *Trends in Cognitive Sciences, 7*(12), 547–552.

18 See, amongst others, the expertise reversal effect described in: Kalyuga, S. (2014). The expertise reversal principle in multimedia learning. *The Cambridge handbook of multimedia learning*, 576–597. Cambridge: Cambridge University Press; and Kalyuga, S., Ayres, P., Chandler, P., & Sweller, J. (2003). The expertise reversal effect. *Educational Psychologist, 38*(1), 23–31.

19 www.learningscientists.org/

10

HAVE A VISION (AND IT DOESN'T MATTER WHICH ONE)

This chapter will explore the following questions:

- Why is it important for a school and a team to have a vision?
- Why is the actual nature of the vision then less important?

Imagine a school that has been constantly written about for more than two years. A school that people visit almost every day to see what the school is actually doing. A school that has both fanatical supporters and opponents. This school is called Michaela and it is in North London. Just mentioning the name of the headmistress, Katharine Birbalsingh, is enough to raise furious debate in British educational circles.

Your first thought might be that Michaela is a school with iPads or, even hipper, virtual reality glasses. But no, the opposite is true. Books are essential to the Michaela philosophy. But the pupils can only read books that are approved by the school. Knowledge and learning are also central, under the motto 'Knowledge is power'.[1] The children learn classical poetry by heart and the school is proud that lessons are given for 59 minutes of each hour. *The Guardian* newspaper calls Michaela the strictest school in the country.[2] Routines are crucial. So is silence: if you make noise, you disturb your fellow pupils in their learning.

By now, you probably think that Michaela is one of those elite public schools for which England is so well known. Perhaps you can see the uniforms, and old 'Harry Potter' style castle and rows of very rich children from very rich homes. True, the pupils at Michaela do wear a uniform, but the school buildings are anything but castle-like. After all, there aren't many castles in one of the poorest parts of London. And it is certainly not an elite 'rich kids' school. Birbalsingh started her school precisely to give children from difficult backgrounds a better chance in life. In June 2017, Michaela was visited by Ofsted, the British school inspection team. The assessment result, much to the amazement of the school's many detractors, was: outstanding.[3]

What is equally remarkable, is that many other schools with a vision and an approach diametrically opposed to Michaela's are also often assessed as being outstanding. Research by Margaret Brown from 2012,[4] which we also discussed in our 'educational myths' book, showed that the supposed polarity between progressive and conservative education is not as evident as many people think, simply because both labels are very difficult to define. Even more important, her study revealed that there were very few differences between schools at both ends of the spectrum.

There are various reasons for this. In practice, teachers are a fairly eclectic bunch and discussions of the 'progressive versus conservative' kind are usually reserved for the policy-makers, whether at national or school board level. But perhaps the most important reason for the similarities between seemingly dissimilar schools is that they have one vital thing in common: they all have a shared vision with clear goals. And the existence of this vision is crucial for learning,[5] perhaps even more crucial than the actual nature of the vision itself.

Why is having a vision so important?

In the previous chapters, we have primarily looked at ways in which teachers can become more meaningful for their pupils and students. But the school and its leadership can also play a key role in improving learning capabilities.[6] In particular, school and classroom climate is a determining factor.[7]

A first reason why a shared school vision is so essential is that it gives pupils and students a certain peace of mind. If a pupil feels that the teacher for the second lesson of the day is a variation on a theme of the teacher for the first lesson, this is reassuring.

The pupils know 'where they are' and this assists learning. This does not mean that teachers cannot be different; far from it. However, things can go wrong if the pupils and students have the feeling in the second lesson that they are sitting in a totally different world from the first lesson, with completely different rules and expectations.

There is also a second reason why a shared vision is so beneficial for pupils and students, although in an indirect way. The presence of a coherent vision about the values for which the school stands, supported and consistently implemented by the school team, is a strong predictor for greater professionalism in that school.[8] This is not illogical: if you all know where you want to go, it is easier to get there and to identify any problems you are likely to meet along the way. In this way, the school vision becomes part of the mental preparation that we described in the chapter about practice. The meta-analyses of Hattie[9] demonstrated that professionalization can have a significant impact on pupil learning.

FURTHER THINKING: EFFECTIVE PROFESSIONALIZATION?

The professionalization of teachers is only effective if it helps their pupils to learn more. Timperley, Wilson, Barrar and Fung[10] investigated which characteristics of professionalization had the most effect on learning in the classroom. Although they found no golden rule, they did reach some significant conclusions:

1. **Professionalization needs time, but just giving time is not enough.** It is also important which time is given (for example, freeing up lesson time is more effective).

2. **It is usually necessary to bring in outside expertise, but this, again, is not enough on its own.** In particular, not every external expert is relevant to the school's situation.

3. **Commitment during the professionalization process is more important than teachers voluntarily undertaking additional training.** The research showed that there is little difference between the effects of voluntary and compulsory training.

4. **The vision present in the school must be challenged.** Although this will only have an effect if repeated regularly.

(Continued)

5. **Participating in a learning community is more important than the where, when and how of this community.** The fact that you can learn and develop yourself as a teacher is more important than whether you do this inside or outside your own school. Learning communities are only effective if they give their participants the opportunity to challenge their own visions and to better understand new and alternative visions, with a clear focus on how their lessons can have an impact on the learning ability of their pupils or students.

6. **The professionalization must be in keeping with broader education policy and the findings of educational research.**

7. **Active leadership at school.** School leaders must work to create an atmosphere in which teachers are able to try out the new things they have learnt during their professionalization trajectory. They must stimulate the development of a learning school and, where necessary, also stimulate others to take the lead.

The huge impact of good leadership on learning at school

In my job as a teacher trainer, I have had the good fortune to be able to visit many schools. It has been my personal experience that you can quickly sense the prevailing atmosphere and also see that the impact of the school management on that atmosphere is huge. The review study by Timperley, Wilson, Barrar and Fung showed that there is a direct correlation between a school vision, professionalization and learning, but only on condition that there is strong leadership from the school director, school management team and school board.

In essence, you could say that a good school director and a good school administration help to ensure that there is a positive learning climate in school,[11] so that the likelihood of a positive leaning climate in the classroom also increases, which in turn leads to better learning.[12] However, in my opinion, this is a two-way process. A good learning environment in the classroom can help to encourage the correct learning environment in the school as a whole, allowing the school director and the school board to breathe a little easier and maybe even sleep at night! Put simply (although less simple to achieve in reality), school directors, management teams, administrators and boards who are able to bind together their teams and are able to ensure that everyone is following the same agreed line are much better able to guide, influence and improve the educational quality of the school. How can you best do this? By setting clear and specific objectives for good educational quality and then taking the necessary action (time and resource provision, training, and so forth) to make these objectives achievable. How can you best *not* do this? By exerting pressure when things go wrong. Instead, offer support and understanding; if you don't, there is a good chance you will lose all confidence and trust.[13]

FURTHER THINKING: WHAT IS A GOOD LEARNING CLIMATE?

In various studies the importance of a positive learning climate has been put forward as a key factor for good learning. But what exactly is a positive or good learning climate? If you compare all the different studies, the following elements consistently reappear over time:[14]

- It is necessary to have order in the class;

- It is necessary to create a feeling of safety in the class;

- It is necessary to have a positive approach towards learning;

- It is necessary to have a positive approach towards pupils;

- It is necessary to have high expectations of pupils;

- It is necessary for pupils to realize that they have both rights and obligations.

Do some visions have more effect than others?

Studies of school culture are often based on effectivity research. If you look at the different international scales used to chart school culture, you will soon notice that they have many features in common. Maslowski[15] has made this comparison and listed the following recurrent elements that contribute to a positive learning culture:

- There is a necessary degree of reflection;
- There is good collaboration between teachers;
- There is a high degree of collegiality;
- There is a necessary degree of vigour and decisiveness in the school;
- There is a necessary level of professional development;
- There is a focus on the learning of the pupils.

This list is very similar to what Tom Bennett described in a more recent review study.[16] Which characteristics do successful schools share? They all have:

- committed, highly visible school leaders, with ambitious goals, supported by a strong leadership team;
- effectively communicated, realistic, detailed expectations understood clearly by all members of the school;
- highly consistent working practices throughout the school;
- a clear understanding of what the school culture is: 'this is how we do things around here, and these are the values we hold';
- high levels of staff and parental commitment to the school vision and strategies;
- high levels of support between leadership and staff; for example, staff training;
- attention to detail and thoroughness in the execution of school policies and strategies;
- high expectations of all students and staff, and a belief that all students matter equally.

If you look closely at both lists, you will see that they set out the necessary features for an effective school organization, an organization that is highly motivated and value driven, but they say very little about the direction in which all that passion and motivation should be channelled. They describe the necessary conditions for having a coherent and shared vision, but say not that much about the nature of the vision itself. So, are there visions that are more or less effective than others? Excluding the more extreme visions, perhaps there are, but these will almost certainly be visions that are not properly embedded in a school culture with the characteristics described above.

FURTHER THINKING: PROBLEMS OF SCALING-UP

If you examine the characteristics of effective schools and note how these characteristics are not dependent on any particular vision, but are more concerned with how an educational team works, you will probably also understand why this makes it so difficult to scale up successful initiatives. Imagine that a school has a revolutionary approach that works brilliantly. So much so, that it seems a good idea to introduce the same approach everywhere. Unfortunately, you will soon discover that this is not as simple as it sounds. Decades of educational reform, often based on this reasoning, have shown, particularly in the United States, that the final result is usually just a pale and ineffective shadow of the original bright idea.[17]

There can be various reasons for this. First and foremost, many of the reforms attempt to change what might be called the 'grammar' of the educational process: a teacher who goes on a journey with a group of pupils, with the intention that the latter will learn something with the help of the former. Reforms that try to tinker with this basic idea soon find that changing something so fundamental is not as easy as you might hope or think.[18]

Secondly, it is sometimes very difficult to know exactly why the original idea was so successful in its original context. Was it the vision? Or was it the passion with which the team worked to implement the vision? Or because the school became the choice of parents who take an especially close interest in the upbringing of their children, which automatically creates a better learning effect? It is often a combination of all three factors or even more, but it is very hard to identify precisely which ones.

If a non-productive approach is introduced by a less passionate or less strongly-led team or in a school where parents are less actively concerned about the upbringing of their children, there is a good chance that the new approach will not be very effective. Worse still, the likelihood that a more productive approach would work at a later stage is also significantly reduced. This is why the two examples of different types of vision in the introduction to this chapter should only be regarded as examples of how you can create a vision, rather than a plea to copy either one or other of them.

But... don't be too fanatical

It is clear that having a shared, coherent vision is important, but at the same time you must ensure that this vision does not hinder teachers from doing what they are paid for: helping pupils to learn. Why are teachers so eclectic? Because good teachers want to do what is best for their pupils, irrespective of doctrine, methods and styles. If they see that one approach is not working, then effective teachers will switch to a different approach that will hopefully do better.

If, as a teacher in the classroom, you stick persistently to the proscriptions of a particular vision 'come what may', this means that you are no longer looking first and foremost at your pupils and what they need. This goes against the principles of everything we have described in this book as 'effective education'. A teacher must be committed to the vision and must stand behind it fully, but they also need to know that it may sometimes be necessary to deviate from it. However, if such deviations become too frequent, this can either mean that the vision is not the right one or that the teacher no longer believes in it. This is the reason why effective schools devote so much attention to reflection. Without reflection, it is not possible to identify, understand and correct situations relating to the proper implementation of the vision.

To cut it short

- It is important as a team that you have a shared vision and coherent vision, so that pupils know where they stand and so that the school as a whole has the necessary atmosphere of calm.
- Whichever vision you choose, it must be subordinate to the needs of the motivation and professionalism of the school team.
- Individual teachers can deviate from the vision, if this is in the learning interest of the child.

Notes

1 http://mcsbrent.co.uk/ethos/
2 www.theguardian.com/education/2016/dec/30/no-excuses-inside-britains-strictest-school
3 www.theguardian.com/teacher-network/2017/jun/16/britains-strictest-school-gets-top-marks-from-ofsted
4 Brown, M. (2012). Traditional versus progressive education. In P. Adey, & J. Dillon (Eds), *Bad education* (pp. 95–110). Maidenhead, UK: Open University Press.
5 Sammons, P., Hillman, J., & Mortimore, P. (1995). *Key characteristics of effective schools: A review of school effectiveness research*. London: Ofsted.

6 There are, of course, numerous other factors that impact on learning: the child themself, their parents, the environment, etc. I am limiting myself here to the educational sphere, because that is where we as educationalists can make a positive contribution.

7 Scheerens, J., (2013). *What is effective schooling? A review of current thought and practice.* Geneva: International Baccalaureate Organization.

8 Kurland, H., Peretz, H., & Hertz-Lazarowitz, R. (2010). Leadership style and organizational learning: the mediate effect of school vision. *Journal of Educational Administration, 48*(1), 7–30.

9 Hattie, 2009.

10 Timperley, H., Wilson, A., Barrar, H., & Fung, I. (2007). *Best evidence synthesis iterations (BES) on professional learning and development.* Wellington, NZ: Ministry of Education.

11 See, amongst others: Deal, T.E., & Peterson, K.D. (2016). *Shaping school culture.* Abingdon: John Wiley & Sons; Levine, D., & Lezotte, L. (1990). *Unusually effective schools: A review of research practice.* Madison, WI: National Center for Effective Schools Research and Development.

12 Amongst other things, the cohesion between the pupils is important. See, amongst others: Mullen, B., & Copper, C. (1994). The relation between group cohesiveness and performance: an integration. *Psychological Bulletin, 115*, 210–227.

13 Hooge, E.H., Janssen, S.K., Look, van K., Moolenaar, N., & Sleegers, P. (2015). *Bestuurlijk vermogen in het primair onderwijs. Mensen verbinden en inhoudelijk op een lijn krijgen om adequaat te sturen op onderwijskwaliteit.* Tilburg: TIAS School for Business and Society, Tilburg University.

14 See, amongst others: Edmonds, R. (1979). Effective schools for the urban poor. *Educational Leadership, 37*, 15–27; Marzano, R.J. (2003). *What works in schools: Translating research into action.* Alexandria, VA: Association for Supervision and Curriculum Development; Marzano, R.J. (2007). Leadership and school reform factors. In T. Townsend (Ed.), *International handbook of school effectiveness and improvement* (pp. 597–614). New York: Springer; Reynolds et al., 2014.

15 Maslowski, R. (2006). A review of inventories for diagnosing school culture. *Journal of Educational Administration, 44*(1), 6–35.

16 Bennett, T. (2017). *Creating a culture: How school leaders can optimise behaviour.* London: Department of Education.

17 Cuban, L. (1992). What happens to reforms that last? The case of the junior high school. *American Educational Research Journal, 29*(2), 227–251.

18 Elmore, R. (1996). Getting to scale with good educational practice. *Harvard Educational Review, 66*(1), 1–27.

11

LIKE YOUR PUPILS

This chapter will explore the following questions:

- Why is it important to work at establishing a good relationship between teacher and pupils?
- What does a good relationship between teacher and pupils look like?
- How can you give shape to a good relationship between teacher and pupils?

If we pay considerable attention to feedback because it has an effect size of 0.73 in John Hattie's *Visible Learning*,[1] you might well ask why we have so far devoted less attention to another aspect of teaching mentioned in the same book with an almost equally large effect; namely, a good relationship between teacher and pupils, with an effect size of 0.72. A more recent meta-analysis described the importance of a good relationship for both pupil commitment and pupil performance.[2] This meta-analysis by Roorda and colleagues also revealed, perhaps contrary to what you might expect, that this relationship becomes even more important as the pupil gets older. In other words, that it is more important for secondary education than for primary education.

This is a purely personal hypothesis, but I feel that the teacher–pupil relationship gets much less attention than feedback because it is much more difficult to frame in terms of rules, training, etc. It is much easier to give a course in 'feedback' than it is to give a course in 'liking your pupils'. Nevertheless, the importance of a good teacher–pupil relationship is huge. Here are just a few concrete examples.

A positive relationship between teachers and pupils in the 10–11-year-old category is a predictor for better behaviour at a later age.

In concrete terms, the researchers found that these pupils were more collaborative and worked more altruistically, while negative problem behaviours, such as aggression, diminished at the same time.[3] Pupils with learning difficulties also benefit from a positive relationship with their teachers, so that they can overcome the learning challenges in the classroom together.[4] The encouragement of the teacher and their belief in their pupils is one of the most strongly influential factors in the learning success of pupils from a difficult background.[5] Conversely, pupils from minority communities are less likely to go on to further education, if they lose trust and confidence in their teachers.[6] Research has similarly indicated that even in nursery schools a positive relationship is important to reduce the stress levels in pre-school age children.[7]

Of course, a good classroom relationship also benefits teachers, although relatively less research has so far been conducted into this aspect. A summary study of the existing corpus by Split and colleagues showed that a good relationship between teachers and pupils can help to enhance the well-being of teachers in the long term, with the opposite also being true: negative pupil behaviour can increase teacher stress, also in part because their mutual relationship comes under greater pressure.[8]

FURTHER THINKING: CLASSROOM CLIMATE

In the previous chapter we talked about the importance of a good school climate.[9] It should be self-evident that a good and positive relationship between teachers and pupils is an important part of that atmosphere. In the Anglo-Saxon world, more attention is devoted in research to the class as a whole. However, in Dutch-language research in Flanders and the Netherlands there is an established tradition of more specifically examining the relationship between the teacher and the pupils being taught.[10]

A number of elements play a role in creating a good classroom climate: the relationship between the pupils themselves, the necessary degree of order, the existence of clearly agreed 'rules' and conditions, appropriate and challenging expectations on the part of the teacher and the wider environment, etc. It is also possible for a school to 'inherit' well-being – and, conversely, ill-being – from outside the school walls. A pupil who is confronted at home with parents who are divorcing will probably also not feel happy at school. If lots of pupils feel this way, for whatever reason, this can have an influence on the class as a whole.

What does a good relationship look like?

If we look at what Theo Wubbels concluded after years of research into this subject, we can see that he focused on three positive attitudes derived from Leary's Rose,[11] a 1957 communication model for behavioural relationships that Wubbels translated to the educational world. According to this model, teacher behaviour can display eight different characteristics. It can be corrective, strict, directing, helping, friendly, understanding, space creating or uncertain and dissatisfied.[12]

As you can see from Figure 11.1, it is primarily the characteristics of nearness that score high in terms of forming a positive relationship between teachers and pupils. However, it needs to be emphasized that this is not the same as becoming friends with your pupils. The necessary degree of distance appropriate to the function of teacher continues to be important.

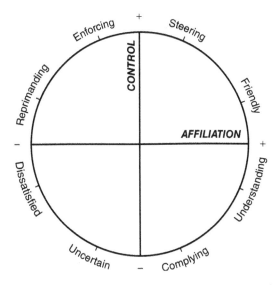

Figure 11.1 Teacher interpersonal circle (Brekelmans et al., 2011)

From my own research and also from research by Wubbels and colleagues,[13] it is clear that teachers who have the courage to take friendly control of the learning process, so that giving direction can be combined with working together, are more likely to develop a good relationship with their pupils and will live up more closely to their pupils' expectations of a 'good' teacher.

How can you work at this kind of relationship?

How can you translate these three 'nearness' characteristics of direction, understanding and friendliness into daily teaching practice? The first thing to note is that it is important to work at these things from the very first day. You sometimes hear it said that it is better 'not to smile in the class before Christmas', but research by Tim Mainhard[14] suggests – and in my opinion correctly – that this advice is dangerous nonsense. The foundations for a good relationship between teacher and pupils must be laid from the very first lessons and then further during the first three months they spend together in class. This is bad news for teachers who are slow starters in this respect, because after this first three months the likelihood of (spontaneous) improvement is small. The message is therefore clear: display the necessary degree of nearness to your pupils from day one and, as Mainhard indicates, show the necessary leadership as the lesson-giver, whilst at the same time being warm and responsive. These latter qualities will ensure that you take proper account of the needs of your pupils and students.

This ties in with a second insight; namely, that as teacher you need to show a positive interest in your pupils, but preferably during informal moments and not during lessons.[15] It is a bad idea to ask a pupil in the middle of a lesson how they are feeling or whether or not they won this weekend at football. But there is no harm in asking these things during the lunch break or on the school playground. Research shows very clearly that these informal interactions reflect very positively on the more formal interaction of the classroom.

This also means that it is advisable not to rush away too quickly after lessons. Stay at your desk and make time for any pupils who want to approach you. To make this possible, school planners should try to ensure that teachers don't always have to run across school to be on time for their next lesson on the other side of the building! This kind of informal moment is also more likely to arise spontaneously when classic lessons are replaced by working in smaller groups, which are inevitably more informal and allow the teacher to show a friendlier side, having first made the necessary eye-contact.[16]

A third option was revealed in research conducted by Gehlbach and colleagues.[17] They reasoned that if pupils are able to discover similarities between themselves and their teachers, this is likely to strengthen their mutual relationship. They carried out a comparative study in which one test group of pupils were told about five things they have in common with the teacher, whereas the control group of pupils were told none of these things. It transpired that the test group not only scored better in class, but also that the gap between children from a difficult background and a normal background became much smaller. More anecdotally, many teachers say that the existence of similarities with their pupils has a positive effect.

Last but not least, trust is crucial to all aspects of the relationship between teacher and pupils. If there is no trust, the relationship will not be a positive one and the pupils will learn relatively little. Cunningham and Resso[18] describe trust as the basis for educational effectivity. Rotter[19] adds that the opportunity to trust someone is an important factor in making learning possible.

How can you work at building trust? In part, you can do this by understanding your pupils' expectations and dealing with them in an appropriate manner.[20] This does not mean that you must always give in to these expectations, but it does mean that you must explain rationally when you do not: 'No, I'm afraid we're not going to end the lesson with a story today, because we've run out of time. But we'll do it as normal next week.'

Other important factors in winning trust are consistent behaviour, clear agreed 'rules', honesty and fair play. And remember: it takes a long while to build up trust but you can lose it in seconds if you do the wrong thing.

FURTHER THINKING: THE IMPORTANCE OF CLASS MANAGEMENT

One of the biggest worries of inexperienced – and often also experienced – teachers is class management.[21] A good relationship with pupils is perhaps a part of this, but the two things are not really the same. In fact, they are both part of the wide concept of classroom and school climate. Dozens of books have been written about class management and the subject really goes beyond the scope of this book. Even so, I would still like to share one or two insights from recent research, since effective

(Continued)

education will not be possible if classes are badly managed or if teachers do not have them under control.[22] Ironically, the best way to keep a class under control is... to give good lessons![23] Fortunately, there are also a number of other useful tips.

Kratochwill, Deroos and Blair[24] describe the conditions necessary to achieve successful class management. They conclude that it is better to focus on what you expect from your pupils in terms of behaviour and learning, rather than concentrating on negative behaviour and how you will punish it. To make this possible, you need to know what behaviour will be necessary to allow successful learning during your lessons. It is therefore useful to ask yourself the following questions before each lesson:

1. **What behaviour is necessary to achieve the objective of the lesson?** When can the pupils be actively involved, when must they listen, when should they look something up?

2. **What role do the pupils need to play in each phase of the lesson?** When can they lead the learning process, when do you as teacher need to do it, who takes what roles in group work?

3. **How as the teacher can I prepare my pupils for all this?** What instructions should I give? What exercises should I give? How can I ensure that everything runs as smoothly as possible? Which routines are important?

Separately from all this, it is necessary that you and your pupils also know how problem behaviour will be dealt with. Finally, a recent meta-analysis[25] has shown that programmes in education that focus on the social-emotional development of pupils generally have a better effect, with a crucial role for the teacher as the person who sees and understands the link between this development and class management.[26]

When can a relationship go wrong?

The Police sang 'Don't stand so close to me' and teachers should take this good advice to heart. You need to be close to your pupils, but not too close. A degree of professional distance remains essential. Even if the relational aspect focuses on learning, too much proximity is wrong. A teacher must always remember that the development of the learner and, by extension, the class, is central.

In this context, fair play is important: if your behaviour towards a particular pupil gives the other pupils the feeling that this is not fair, your relationship of trust with the majority will come under increasing pressure, which can have a negative impact on learning effectiveness.[27] This idea of fairness can also be useful in helping you, as the teacher, to answer difficult questions. For example, is it a good idea to become 'friends' with pupils on social media, like Facebook. If you are 'friends' with only two or three of your pupils, is this really fair on all the others? Probably not, so either give everyone the same chance or no one. Of course, fair does not mean that you always have to treat everyone exactly the same. Fair can also mean that you give a pupil with learning difficulties extra support.

To cut it short

- Like your pupils and build up a good relationship with them: this can have a huge impact on learning effectiveness.
- Being liked as a teacher means showing appropriate behaviour that is directing, friendly and supportive.
- Keep your distance and treat all pupils fairly.

Notes

1 Hattie, 2009.
2 Roorda, D.L., Koomen, H.M., Spilt, J.L., & Oort, F.J. (2011). The influence of affective teacher–student relationships on students' school engagement and achievement: a meta-analytic approach. *Review of Educational Research*, *81*(4), 493–529.
3 Obsuth, I., et al. (2016). A non-bipartite propensity score analysis of the effects of teacher–student relationships on adolescent problem and prosocial behavior. *Journal of Youth and Adolescence*. DOI 10.1007/s10964-016-0534-y.
4 Al-Yagon, M. (2012). Adolescents with learning disabilities: socioemotional and behavioral functioning and attachment relationships with fathers, mothers, and teachers. *Journal of Youth and Adolescence*, *41*, 1294–1311.
5 Alcott, B.M. (2017). Does teacher encouragement influence students' educational progress? A propensity-score matching analysis. *Research in Higher Education*. DOI 10.1007/s11162-017-9446-2.
6 Yeager, D.S., Purdie-Vaughns, V., Hooper, S.Y., & Cohen, G.L. (2017). Loss of institutional trust among racial and ethnic minority adolescents: a consequence of procedural injustice and a cause of life-span outcomes. *Child Development*, *88*(2), 658–676.

7   Hatfield, B.E., & Williford, A.P. (2017). Cortisol patterns for young children displaying disruptive behavior: links to a teacher–child, relationship-focused intervention. *Prevention Science: The Official Journal of the Society for Prevention Research*, *18*(1), 40–49.

8   Spilt, J.L., Koomen, H.M., & Thijs, J.T. (2011). Teacher wellbeing: the importance of teacher–student relationships. *Educational Psychology Review*, *23*(4), 457–477.

9   Berkowitz, R., Moore, H., Astor, R.A., & Benbenishty, R. (2017). A research synthesis of the associations between socioeconomic background, inequality, school climate, and academic achievement. *Review of Educational Research*, *87*(2), 425–469.

10 Wubbels, T. (2014). Leraar-leerlingrelaties in de klas: toekomst voor onderzoek. *Pedagogische Studiën*, *91*, 352–363.

11 Leary, T. (1957). *An interpersonal diagnosis of personality*. New York: The Ronald Press Company.

12 In the original version from 1984, the diagram represented a rose, but is now more like a circle. Compare Créton & Wubbels, 1984 (Créton, H.A., & Wubbels, T. (1984). *Ordeproblemen bij beginnende leraren*. Utrecht: WCC.), with this updated version: Van, J., Mainhard, T., Brekelmans, M., Den Brok, P., & Levy, J. (2014). Docent-leerling interacties en het sociaal klimaat in de klas. In J. Van Tartwijk, M. Brekelmans, P. Den Brok & T. Mainhard (Eds), *Theorie en praktijk van leren en de leraar: Liber Amicorum Theo Wubbels* (pp. 25-43). Amsterdam: Uitgeverij SWP.

13 See: Wubbels, Th., Brekelmans, M., & Hooymayers, H.P. (1993). Comparison of teachers' and students' perceptions of interpersonal teacher behavior. In T. Wubbels, & J. Levy (Eds), *Do you know what you look like?* (pp. 64–80). London, UK: Falmer Press; Wubbels, Th., Brekelmans, M., den Brok, P., & Tartwijk, J. van (2006). An interpersonal perspective on classroom management in secondary classrooms in the Netherlands. In C. Evertson & C. Weinstein (Eds), *Handbook of classroom management: Research, practice, and contemporary issues* (pp. 1161–1192). Mahwah, NJ: Lawrence Erlbaum.

14 Mainhard, M.T., Brekelmans, M., den Brok, P., & Wubbels, T. (2011). The development of the classroom social climate during the first months of the school year. *Contemporary Educational Psychology*, *36*(3), 190–200.

15 This was partly in evidence in my own research (De Bruyckere & Kirschner, 2016) but has also been found in research conducted in other regions (for example, Johnson, Z.D., & La Belle, S. (2017). An examination of teacher authenticity in the college classroom. *Communication Education*, *66*(4), 423–439).

16 Marreveld, M. (2014). Een Meester Neemt Afscheid. *Didactief*

17 Gehlbach, H., et al. (2016). Creating birds of similar feathers: leveraging similarity to improve teacher–student relationships and academic achievement. *Journal of Educational Psychology, 108*(3), 342.

18 Cunningham, W.G., & Gresso, D.W. (1993). *Cultural leadership: The culture of excellence in education*. Boston, MA: Allyn & Bacon.

19 Rotter, J.B. (1967). A new scale for the measurement of interpersonal trust. *Journal of Personality, 35*(4), 651–665.

20 De Bruyckere, P. (2017). *Authenticity Lies in the Eye of the Beholder*. Doctoral Thesis, Heerlen: Open Universiteit.

21 Dicke, T., Elling, J., Schmeck, A., & Leutner, D. (2015). Reducing reality shock: the effects of classroom management skills training on beginning teachers. *Teaching and Teacher Education, 48*, 1–12.

22 Jones, V.F., & Jones, L.S. (2012). *Comprehensive classroom management, creating communities of support and solving problems* (10th edn). Upper Saddle River, NJ: Pearson.

23 Slavin, R.E. (2012). *Educational psychology: Theory and practice*. Upper Saddle River, NJ: Pearson.

24 Kratochwill, T., DeRoos, R., & Blair, S. (2014). What works in classroom management. In R.E. Slavin (Ed.), *Proven programs in education: Classroom management and assessment*. Thousand Oaks, CA: Corwin Press.

25 Korpershoek, H., Harms, T., de Boer, H., van Kuijk, M., & Doolaard, S. (2016). A meta-analysis of the effects of classroom management strategies and classroom management programs on students' academic, behavioral, emotional, and motivational outcomes. *Review of Educational Research, 86*(3), 643–680.

26 Jones, S.M., Bailey, R., & Jacob, R. (2014). Social-emotional learning is essential to classroom management. *Phi Delta Kappan, 96*(2), 19–24.

27 The concept and importance of fair play in education comes from conversations I had with Maarten Simons (KULeuven).

12

UNDERLYING THEMES

This chapter will revisit key themes from across the book.

When writing this book, I soon began to realize that a number of themes kept recurring, sometimes more obviously, sometimes under the surface. It may be useful to end the book by highlighting and clarifying all these underlying themes. They are not specific tools as such, but are more a series of insights that play a key role in the use of the different tools. By making these underlying themes explicit, I hope not only to add an additional weapon to your educational armoury, but also to give you the benefits of repetition, which we saw in Chapter 5.

Students often don't know what is best for them...

Yes, of course, you must listen to your pupils. Pupils are important, obviously. At the same time, it became apparent to me at different points in the book that pupils do not always know what is best for them.[1] Perhaps they think that self-discovery learning is more fun, but they learn less.[2] They probably feel that taking misconceptions as a starting point is less fun, but they learn more.[3] Think back, for example, to the chapter on deliberate practice.

Metacognition is another area where children and young people find it hard to make an accurate assessment of themselves, although this can vary from subject to subject and study field to study field.[4] Generally speaking, pupils tend to overestimate their own level of knowledge, how well they perform in tests and the speed with which they can complete a learning task. Such optimistic estimations (and negative ones as well) can hinder learning.[5]

Be honest: how often have you thought 'This will only take an hour', when in reality it took twice as long! And how often have you said 'This time I'm really going to plan things properly', but when the moment actually came...? Exactly! But there is good news: you are not the only one. For beginners in any study field it is extremely hard to estimate how difficult something will be or how long it will take. The more the pupils grow in the field of study, the better their estimating skills become and the more their metacognition will develop. But before you get that far, you first need someone who can help you to estimate more accurately. And that someone is called the teacher.

This has important consequences for what you do before, during and after your lessons. Beforehand, you need to be clear about your expectations, say how much time you think the task will take and point out the potential difficulties. During the task (or learning process), you should monitor as far as possible how things are progressing: where the pupils are getting stuck, where things are going well, and so on. You will also need to check how focused they remain on the task. Sometimes this can be difficult; for example, on housework or home study. Hence the importance afterwards of a good feedback process. When giving feedback, it is vital not only to assess the extent to which objective of the task or learning process has been achieved (product), but also how and why the learner was able to reach this objective (or not). This also means asking, for example, whether or not the pupil began the task on time, and what they did if there was something that they did not understand.[6] In doing all this, however, you also need to take account of our following underlying theme; namely working towards objectives.

Work towards objectives

This is an aspect that recurs regularly throughout the book: always work towards specific objectives. Objectives are important to understand why you do what you do and to know where you want to go. This helps the pupils to make mental visualizations and allows both teacher and pupils to identify areas where everything is going according to plan and areas that still need to be worked on. You can't give effective feedback if you don't set objectives.

So what do we know about lesson objectives?

- They should be focused on the short term;
- They should be as specific as possible;
- They should be challenging enough, but also feasible.

If you formulate your objectives in this way, you will enhance the motivation of your pupils and students. Objectives focused on the long term are usually very general and too challenging, which means they are less motivating and work less well.[7]

FURTHER THINKING: 10 INSTRUCTIONAL PRINCIPLES FOR TEACHERS

Barack Rosenshine[8] noted the following principles that every teacher should know. So how many do you recognize?

1. Repeat each day part of what had already been learnt.

2. Present new material in small chunks and help the pupils to practise them.

3. Ask lots of questions, particularly 'how' and 'why' questions; this not only helps pupils to learn but also allows you to see how far along they are in the learning process.

4. Act as a model; demonstrate your own thought and work processes when solving problems.

5. Offer support for difficult tasks (see Chapter 3 on scaffolding).

6. Direct and guide pupils in their practice of new material; just showing it once is not enough.

7. Check regularly that the pupils have understood properly.

8. Make sure the pupils show their successes, so that you can see this and correct, if necessary.

9. Demand and monitor independent practice and work towards this all the time.

10. Regularly activate learned knowledge through a wide range of different exercises.

Transfer is difficult

Learning generic skills is important. Skills that you can use every-where. Just imagine it: you learn a skill in one subject, for example, how to make summaries, and then you can automatically use the same skill in every other subject. That has long been a dream in edu-cation and we call this dream 'transfer'. But like most dreams it is difficult to realize. We know that we want transfer, but we also know that it seldom happens spontaneously.[9]

First of all, let's be clear: not all transfer is difficult. Many of the basic skills that children learn in primary education are easily transferable. For example, the ability to read and write is not only used in language sub-jects. The ability to 'do sums' is also used in physics, chemistry, and other scientific subjects. No, the real challenge begins once you move beyond the transfer of these basic skills.

Throughout the book, we have seen on repeated occasions that the learning of generic skills, skills that you can apply everywhere, is by no means easy. This was clear in the chapter on learning to learn and metacognition, where was saw individual subjects offer few handles to make transfer possible. It is better to work with metacognition directly in the subject that needs to be learnt.

But no matter how difficult it is to transfer more complex skills, for-tunately it is not impossible. For example, the testing effect (the repeated testing of pupils as part of their guidance and learning) is known to increase the likelihood of transfer. Research has also con-firmed the importance for teachers and teams to make clear to pupils where possible skill links to other subjects exist.

This is not a plea for subject-based education in preference to integrated education. Even so, it is clear that learning is context-related. Transferring insights from one context to another must be learnt, often insight by insight.[10]

Rhythm is important

Not too fast, not too slow. This is a variation on the theme mentioned earlier in the book about ensuring that the tasks you set your pupils are not too easy, but also not too hard. Rhythm involves looking at your pupils and giving them the right challenges at the right moment. You need to know when you should slow down or speed up.

But rhythm is more than just setting the pace at which learning progresses. This entire book is an appeal for the necessary variation in education and didactic methods. There is no 'magic' technique or techniques that you can use at all times and in all places. Part of the professionalism of being a teacher involves knowing when to use the right technique at the right time for the right purpose. For example, direct instruction works better than problem-oriented education for the acquisition of basic knowledge, whereas problem-oriented education works better to fix and develop that basic knowledge once it has been acquired. This is why I argued in the first chapter for the importance of continuing to broaden your repertoire as a teacher, since this will not only give your lessons much needed and essential variation, but will also allow you to pick the right approach for the right circumstances.

FURTHER THINKING: INTERLEAVING

One of the six study tips summarized by the Learning Scientists in their *Six Strategies for Effective Learning* poster[11] is also about rhythm and variation, specifically about the alternation of the things that you learn. This is known as interleaving.[12]
   Concrete tips include:

- Change the subject regularly during the study period. Don't stay on the same subject for too long.

- Change the order in which you study the different lesson subjects, since this will strengthen your understanding.

But there are also two warnings:

- Variation is good, but don't overdo it. Changing too often, so that you devote too little time to a subject, can hamper your learning. It is crucial to understand what you are studying.

- Different types of content can sometimes interfere with each other. If you first learn 20 words of Spanish and then 20 words of French, the chances are you will remember both less well.

The Matthew effect

One of the major challenges in education is the elimination of the effect of inequality. In the chapter about the importance of knowledge,

I explained how two children with similar levels of intelligence could achieve different outcomes as a result of the different life experiences they had undergone. Even if all children were able to grow up in ideal circumstances, there would still be a gulf caused by hereditary factors. But if, as previously mentioned, the circumstances of their upbringing are 'sub-optimal', the influence of their environment on learning inevitably becomes greater in a negative sense.

Many of the measures you can take in education suffer from what is known as the Matthew effect: they have a more positive effect on pupils from a strong and stable background than on pupils from families with a low social-economic status (SES). As a result, inequality continues to increase.[13] Take, for example, the idea of adding extra time at school to allow more learning to take place. A 2014 meta-study revealed that allowing more time would have a positive effect for certain groups of pupils, which sounds good.[14] But there is an important catch: if you give everyone the same amount of extra time, the pupils from a strong background will learn proportionally more than pupils from a weaker background.[15]

A variant of the same problem also arises if we look at the idea of shortening the long summer holiday. According to John Hattie, the effect of the long summer holiday is *on average* negative, with an *average* negative effect size of –0.09.[16] Teachers will probably notice this in practice. After the summer holidays, you soon realize that some of the pupils and students have forgotten a lot of what they learned during the previous school year. But it is no coincidence that I used the word 'average' twice. Averages are made up from highs and lows, and research has shown that the effect of long summer holidays on children from families with a low SES is significantly more negative than the average, whereas the effect on children from families with a higher SES is significantly more positive than the average, presumably because their circumstances make it easier for them to continue making use of their previously learnt knowledge during the holiday period. A similar phenomenon (but in the opposite direction) can also be observed in the so-called expertise reversal effect. This occurs when a particular educational method works well for children with little prior knowledge but loses its effectiveness when used on children with lots of prior knowledge.

So what can be done to close these gulfs in equality?

I have already mentioned the benefits of direct instruction for the learning of basic knowledge. And this is true, the gulf is effectively made smaller but without the smart pupils losing out. However, this latter group can eventually be affected by the expertise reversal effect if the direct instruction method continues to be used for too long after they have acquired the basic knowledge they need.[17] The previously mentioned meta-study about extra lesson and learning time at school also revealed that this would work most to the benefit of children from a weaker background, providing these extra lessons were predominantly directive (i.e. teacher-led).

Another recent meta-analysis by Jens Dietrichson et al.[18] has also identified approaches that can help to close the equality gap, although at the same time they issue a number of caveats or warnings:

- No single approach will ever completely close the gap between children from low SES families and high SES families, although the more effective approaches will narrow that gap.
- For some of the approaches just under the 'top four', it is possible that their seemingly lesser effect may be a consequence of the limited number of studies to which they have been subjected.

The top four approaches that can make a difference are:

- **Tutoring**, in which pupils receive extra help from a tutor or mentor. This additional guidance can be given individually or in small groups of a maximum of five pupils. The tutors can either be paid professional teachers or unpaid volunteers.
- **Feedback and monitoring of learning progress:** see the chapter on feedback and the link to direct instruction.
- **Instruction in smaller groups**, in which pupils are taught in groups smaller than the usual class size but larger than the tutor groups of a maximum of five pupils.
- **Cooperative learning:** this is learning together, but is essentially different from normal group work. Pupils work in duos or small groups to solve problems in a systematic and structured way. Stronger pupils can be used in this method to assist their weaker classmates.

Then, of course, there is the most important factor of all: good teachers giving good lessons. As explained in Chapter 3 and elsewhere, it is vital for teachers to have and maintain a good level of professional knowledge, as well as the ability to translate that knowledge to the level of their pupils and students, particularly those who come from more difficult backgrounds.

A final underlying theme: Cognitive load theory

A final element that appeared in several chapters of this book is a theory that Dylan Wiliam referred to on Twitter as the most important theory to understand the essence of education: John Sweller's cognitive load theory.[19] Having said that, it is necessary to remember – as Paul Kirschner has rightly pointed out[20] – that this is a theory and not a didactic instrument. And as a theory, it has both supporters and opponents.

Why do I want to highlight this theory again? Because in my opinion it helps to explain why different didactic approaches mentioned in the book work well, when others do not. What is the starting point for cognitive load theory? In short, it states that there is a bottleneck in our memory system. This bottleneck means that information is sometimes not easily stored in our brain, although fortunately there are tricks that allow us to use the bottleneck as effectively as possible.

On one side of the bottleneck we receive lots of stimuli via our senses, which are briefly stored in our sensory memory. This sensory memory has a high storage capacity and can hold information for several seconds. So this is not the bottleneck. On the other side of the bottleneck sits our long-term memory. The name says it all: this is the place where information is stored for longer periods and its capacity is seemingly limitless. According to Sweller's theory, this is where everything we remember is filed away in memory banks. So this is not the bottleneck, either.

Imagine that all the information in the sensory memory could be transferred directly to the long-term memory. If this was possible, we would remember a huge amount, but probably too much. For this reason, the brain has inserted a third memory as a bottleneck between these two memories. This is known as the short-term memory or working memory.

This working memory only has a limited capacity, which means that stimuli in the sensory memory that are not processed quickly are automatically removed from the system. This information overload of the working memory is central to the cognitive load theory.

According to the theory, there are three types of cognitive overload.[21]

- Intrinsic (inherent) overload: this is mental overload that is linked to the things you are trying to learn, and more particularly with the complexity of what needs to be learnt. What determines this level of complexity? Amongst other things, how many different elements need to be learnt. If you want to learn 20 words in a foreign language, this will be less complex than learning how to use those 20 words in sentences. Loose words with no connections are much simpler than words incorporated into sentences, where you need to take account of grammar, interactions, etc.
- Extraneous (irrelevant) overload: this is mental overload that has nothing to do with the subject matter you are trying to learn, but still attracts part of your attention. Just try and enjoy a concert if you have the nagging feeling that you haven't turned the gas off at home!
- Germane (useful) overload: this is mental overload that benefits the learning process and ensures that what you have learnt is stored in schedules in the memory banks of the long-term memory.

What can you do as a teacher to make sure that as much useful information as possible passes through the bottleneck of the working memory?

You can reduce intrinsic overload by splitting up complex subjects into smaller parts. We saw this earlier in the book in the chapter on deliberate practice, but also in the section on Rosenshine's second principle of instruction, which says that new material is best offered to pupils and students step by step in small pieces, supported by regular repetition and practice.

However, it is even more important to minimize irrelevant overload and maximize germane overload. We have looked at numerous examples earlier in the book, such as the importance of not overloading the dual channel system in the working memory, or Mayer's redundancy principle in the chapter on multimedia learning. Information can pass easily through the bottleneck if words and images are combined, but the use of too many stimuli – for example, the combination of written and spoken text – can actually reduce the amount of learning, by blocking the bottleneck with too many things at once. Similarly, images that have nothing to do with the subject matter also deflect learning attention, by channelling unnecessary information into the bottleneck, so that more useful data are unable to pass.

The chapter on prior knowledge also has useful tips on how you can get the right information through the bottleneck. Following Geake, I described the working memory as the brain's spam filter. Translated to the cognitive load theory, this means that prior knowledge ensures that stimuli in the sensory memory can be more easily identified, so that they are processed more quickly and transferred through to the long-term memory.

Automation, repetition and practice are three other effective techniques for the reduction of irrelevant overload. Do you remember the example about what it would mean if you had to think from scratch every time you stand before a closed door? If you can automate information in your mind, this enables you to do things without thinking (or rather without consciously thinking). In this way, you place less pressure on the working memory.

With a little bit of imagination, you might even say that metacognition is, amongst other things, about how you can find ways to avoid cognitive (over)load by, for example, not studying for too long at any one sitting, learning how to use mnemonic tricks or by applying some of the many other study tips mentioned in the course of the book.

Some sources of irrelevant overload are difficult to eliminate. We have seen how Mullainathan and Shafir[22] demonstrated that stress can narrow the mental waveband. Hattie and Yates[23] also refer to stress as the most common cause of reduced levels of attention. This stress is not frequently to be found in the actual learning environment, although the school itself can sometimes be a source of unwanted pressure. Schools can help to reduce this by broadening the mental waveband wherever possible, by deflecting attention away from the elements that cause stress and pressure,[24] in part by developing the good relationships we referred to in the previous chapter or by teaching children and young people how to deal with these negative elements in a constructive manner.

But perhaps the most important way that teachers and schools can ensure that the working memory is used to optimal effect is simply to give excellent lessons. This means clear goals, good instruction, good learning materials, enough variation, enough breaks, quality feedback and, above all, just liking the pupils and students you teach.

Notes

1 Kirschner, P.A., & van Merriënboer, J.J. (2013). Do learners really know best? Urban legends in education. *Educational Psychologist*, *48*(3), 169–183.
2 See Chapter 2.
3 See Chapter 4.
4 Dunning, D. (2005). *Self-insight: Roadblocks and detours on the path to knowing thyself*. New York, NY: Psychology Press.
5 Ehrlinger, J., & Shain, E.A. (2014). *How accuracy in students' self-perceptions relates to success in learning*. In: Benassi, V.A., Overson, C.E., & Hakala, C.M. (Eds), *Applying science of learning in education: infusing psychological science into the curriculum*. Retrieved from the Society for the Teaching of Psychology website: http://teachpsych.org/ebooks/asle2014/index.php
6 Hattie & Yates, 2013.
7 See, amongst others: Anderman, E.M., & Wolters, C. (2006). Goals, values and affect: influences on student motivation. In P.A. Alexander & P. Winne (Eds), *Handbook of educational psychology* (2nd edn, pp. 369–389). Mahwah, NJ: Erlbaum; Locke, E.A., & Latham, G.P. (2002). Building a practically useful theory of goal setting and task motivation: a 35-year odyssey. *American Psychologist*, *57*, 705–717; Martin, A.J. (2013). Goal setting and personal best (PB) goals. In J. Hattie & E.M. Anderman (Eds), *International guide to student achievement* (pp. 356–358). New York, NY: Routledge.
8 Rosenshine, 2012.
9 Simons, P.R.J., & Verschaffel, L. (1992). Transfer: onderzoek en onderwijs. *Tijdschrift voor onderwijsresearch*, *17*(1), 3–16.
10 American Psychological Association. (2015). Top 20 principles from psychology for pre K-12 teaching and learning.
11 Check out the posters here: www.learningscientists.org/
12 Rohrer, D. (2012). Interleaving helps students distinguish among similar concepts. *Educational Psychology Review*, *24*, 355–367.

13 Walberg, H.J., & Tsai, S.L. (1983). Matthew effects in education. *American Educational Research Journal, 20*(3), 359–373.

14 Kidron, Y., & Lindsay, J. (2014). *The effects of increased learning time on student academic and nonacademic outcomes: findings from a meta-analytic review*. REL 2014-015. Regional Educational Laboratory Appalachia.

15 Hayes, M.S., & Gershenson, S. (2016). What differences a day can make: quantile regression estimates of the distribution of daily learning gains. *Economics Letters, 141*, 48–51.

16 Hattie, 2009.

17 Kalyuga, S. (2007). Expertise reversal effect and its implications for learner-tailored instruction. *Educational Psychology Review, 19*(4), 509–539.

18 Dietrichson, J., Bøg, M., Filges, T., & Kling Jørgensen, A.M. (2017). Academic interventions for elementary and middle school students with low socioeconomic status: a systematic review and meta-analysis. *Review of Educational Research, 87*(2), 243–282.

19 Sweller, J. (1988). Cognitive load during problem solving: effects on learning. *Cognitive Science, 12*(2), 257–285.

20 https://onderzoekonderwijs.net/2016/01/03/cognitieve-belasting-the-orie-leuker-kunnen-we-het-maken-en-ook-makkelijker/

21 Sweller, J., Van Merriënboer, J.J., & Paas, F.G. (1998). Cognitive architecture and instructional design. *Educational Psychology Review, 10*(3), 251–296.

22 Mullanaitan & Shafir, 2013.

23 Hattie & Yates, 2013.

24 De Bruyckere & Simons, 2016.

REFERENCES

Abadzi, H. (2008). Efficient learning for the poor: new insights into literacy acquisition for children. *International Review of Education, 54*(5–6), 581–604.

Aben, B., Stapert, S., & Blokland, A. (2013). Kortetermijngeheugen en werkgeheugen: Zinnig of dubbelzinnig? *Tijdschrift voor neuropsychologie, 8*(2).

Adesope, O.O., & Nesbit, J.C. (2012). Verbal redundancy in multimedia learning environments. *Journal of Educational Psychology, 104*(1), 250–263.

Adesope, O.O., Trevisan, D.A., & Sundararajan, N. (2017). Rethinking the use of tests: a meta-analysis of practice testing. *Review of Educational Research*, 0034654316689306.

Al-Yagon, M. (2012). Adolescents with learning disabilities: socioemotional and behavioral functioning and attachment relationships with fathers, mothers, and teachers. *Journal of Youth and Adolescence, 41*, 1294–1311.

Alcott, B.M. (2017). Does teacher encouragement influence students' educational progress? A propensity-score matching analysis. *Research in Higher Education*. DOI 10.1007/s11162-017-9446-2

Alvermann, D.E., Smith, L.C., & Readence, J.E. (1985). Prior knowledge activation and the comprehension of compatible and incompatible text. *Reading Research Quarterly, 20*, 420–436.

Ambrose, S.A., Bridges, M.W., DiPietro, M., Lovett, M.C., & Norman, M.K. (2010). *How learning works: Seven research-based principles for smart teaching*. Abingdon: John Wiley & Sons.

American Psychological Association (2015). Top 20 principles from psychology for pre K-12 teaching and learning.

Anderman, E.M., & Wolters, C. (2006). Goals, values, and affect: influences on student motivation. In P.A. Alexander & P. Winne (Eds), *Handbook of educational psychology* (2nd edn, pp. 369–389). Mahwah, NJ: Erlbaum.

Askew, M., Rhodes, V., Brown, M., William, D., & Johnson, D. (1994). Effective teachers of numeracy. *Report of a study carried out for the Teacher Training Agency*. London: King's College London, School of Education.

Austin, K.A. (2009). Multimedia learning: cognitive individual differences and display design techniques predict transfer learning with multimedia learning modules. *Computers & Education*, *53*(4), 1339–1354.

Ausubel, D.P. (1960). The use of advance organizers in the learning and retention of meaningful verbal material. *Journal of Educational Psychology*, *51*, 267–272.

Ausubel, D.P., Novak, J.D., & Hanesian, H. (1968). *Educational psychology: A cognitive view*. New York: Holt, Rinehart and Winston Inc.

Bacon, F. (2000). *Novum organum* (L. Jardine & M. Silverthorne, Trans.). Cambridge, UK: Cambridge University Press. (Original work published in 1620.)

Bakermans, J., Franzen, Y., Hoof, N. van, Veenman, S., & Boer, G. de (1997). *Effectieve instructie in het voortgezet onderwijs. Leren onderwijzen met behulp van het directe instructiemodel*. Amersfoort: CPS.

Bangert-Drowns, R.L., Hurley, M.M., & Wilkinson, B. (2004). The effects of school-based writing-to-learn interventions on academic achievement: a meta-analysis. *Review of Educational Research*, *74*(1), 29–58.

Barrett, T. (2005) What is problem-based learning?' In G. O'Neill, S. Moore, & B. McMullin (Eds), *Emerging issues in the practice of university learning and teaching*. Dublin: All Ireland Society for Higher Education (AISHE).

BBC (2010). *The Classroom Experiment*. London: BBC.

Benjamin, A.S., & Pashler, H. (2015). The value of standardized testing: a perspective from cognitive psychology. *Policy Insights from the Behavioral and Brain Sciences*, *2*(1), 13–23.

Bennett, T. (2017). *Creating a culture: How school leaders can optimise behaviour*. London: Department of Education. Retrieved from https://www.gov.uk/government/uploads/system/uploads/attachment_data/file/602487/Tom_Bennett_Independent_Review_of_Behaviour_in_Schools.pdf.

Berkowitz, R., Moore, H., Astor, R.A., & Benbenishty, R. (2017). A research synthesis of the associations between socioeconomic background, inequality, school climate, and academic achievement. *Review of Educational Research*, *87*(2), 425–469.

Bernard, R.M., Brauer, A., Abrami, P.C., & Surkes, M. (2004). The development of a questionnaire for predicting online learning achievement. *Distance Education*, *25*(1), 31–47.

Bjork, R.A., & Bjork, E.L. (1992). A new theory of disuse and an old theory of stimulus fluctuation. In A. Healy, S. Kosslyn, & R. Shiffrin (Eds), *From learning processes to cognitive processes: Essays in honor of William K. Estes* (Vol. 2, pp. 35–67). Hillsdale, NJ: Erlbaum.

Black, P., & Wiliam, D. (2010). Inside the black box: raising standards through classroom assessment. *Phi Delta Kappan*, *92*(1), 81–90.

Brekelmans, J.M.G., Mainhard, T., Brok, den, P.J., & Wubbels, T. (2011). Teacher control and affiliation: do students and teachers agree? *Journal of Classroom Interaction*, 46(1), 17–26.

Brown, M. (2012). Traditional versus progressive education. In P. Adey, & J. Dillon (Eds), *Bad education* (pp. 95–110). Maidenhead, UK: Open University Press.

Bruner, J. (1972). *Play: Its role in development and evolution*. Harmondsworth: Penguin.

Butler, A.C., Fazio, L.K., & Marsh, E.J. (2011). The hypercorrection effect persists over a week, but high-confidence errors return. *Psychonomic Bulletin & Review*, 18(6), 1238–1244.

Camerer, C., Loewenstein, G., & Weber, M. (1989). The curse of knowledge in economic settings: an experimental analysis. *Journal of Political Economy*, 97(5), 1232–1254.

Carless, D. (2006). Differing perceptions in the feedback process. *Studies in Higher Education*, 31(2), 219–233.

Carpenter, S.K. (2012). Testing enhances the transfer of learning. *Current Directions in Psychological Science*, 21(5), 279–283.

Castelijns, J., Segers, M., & Struyven, K. (2011). *Evalueren om te leren. Toetsen en beoordelen op school*. Coutinho: Bussum.

Castro, M., Expósito-Casas, E., López-Martín, E., Lizasoain, L., Navarro-Asencio, E., & Gaviria, J.L. (2015). Parental involvement on student academic achievement: a meta-analysis. *Educational Research Review*, 14, 33–46.

Center on the Developing Child at Harvard University (2014). *Enhancing and practicing executive function skills with children from infancy to adolescence*. Retrieved from www.developingchild.harvard.edu.

Chaiklin, S. (2003). The zone of proximal development in Vygotsky's analysis of learning and instruction. *Vygotsky's Educational Theory in Cultural Context*, 1, 39–64.

Clark, R.C., & Mayer, R.E. (2016). *E-learning and the science of instruction: Proven guidelines for consumers and designers of multimedia learning*. Abingdon: John Wiley & Sons.

Conway, A.R.A. (2003). Working memory capacity and its relation to general intelligence. *Trends in Cognitive Sciences*, 7(12), 547–552.

Cooper, H. (1989). *Homework*. White Plains, NY: Longman.

Craik, F.I.M., & Lockhart, R.S. (1972). Levels of processing: a framework for memory research. *Journal of Verbal Learning and Verbal Behavior*, 11, 671–684.

Créton, H.A., & Wubbels, T. (1984). *Ordeproblemen bij beginnende leraren*. Utrecht: WCC.

Cuban, L. (1992). What happens to reforms that last? The case of the junior high school. *American Educational Research Journal*, 29(2), 227–251.

Cunningham, W.G., & Gresso, D.W. (1993). *Cultural leadership: The culture of excellence in education*. Boston, MA: Allyn & Bacon.

d'Ydewalle, G., & Pavakanun, U. (1995). *Acquisition of a second/foreign language by viewing a television program*. In P. Winterhoff-Spurk (Ed.), *Psychology of media in Europe: The state of the art – perspectives for the future* (pp. 51–64). Opladen, Germany: Westdeutscher Verlag GmbH.

d'Ydewalle, G., & Van de Poel, M. (1999). Incidental foreign-language acquisition by children watching subtitled television programs. *Journal of Psycholinguistic Research, 28*, 227–244.

Danan, M. (1992). Reversed subtitling and dual coding theory: new directions for foreign language instruction. *Language Learning, 42*(4), 497–527.

Deal, T.E., & Peterson, K.D. (2016). *Shaping school culture*. Abingdon: John Wiley & Sons.

De Block, A., & Heene, J. (1986). *Inleiding tot de algemene didactiek*. Standaard.

De Block, A. & Heene, J. (1993). *De school en haar doelstellingen*. Antwerpen: Standaard Educatieve Uitgeverij.

De Bruyckere, P. (2017). *Authenticity lies in the eye of the beholder*. Doctoral Thesis, Heerlen: Open Universiteit.

De Bruyckere, P., & Kirschner, P.A. (2016). Authentic teachers: Student criteria perceiving authenticity of teachers. *Cogent Education, 3*(1), 1247609. https://doi.org/10.1080/2331186X.2016.1247609.

De Bruyckere, P., & Simons, M. (2016). Scarcity at school. *European Educational Research Journal, 15*(2), 260–267.

De Bruyckere, P., Kirschner, P.A., & Hulshof, C.D. (2015). *Urban myths about learning and education*. Cambridge, MA: Academic Press.

Decroly, O., & Boon, G. (1921). Vers l'école rénovée: une première étape. Paris: Librairie Fernand Nathan.

Dicke, T., Elling, J., Schmeck, A., & Leutner, D. (2015). Reducing reality shock: the effects of classroom management skills training on beginning teachers. *Teaching and Teacher Education, 48*, 1–12.

Dietrichson, J., Bøg, M., Filges, T., & Klint Jørgensen, A.M. (2017). Academic interventions for elementary and middle school students with low socioeconomic status: A systematic review and meta-analysis. *Review of Educational Research, 87*(2), 243–282.

Dignath, C., & Büttner, G. (2008). Components of fostering self-regulated learning among students: a meta-analysis on intervention studies at primary and secondary school level. *Metacognition and Learning, 3*(3), 231–264.

Dolmans, D.H., Gijselaers, W.H., Moust, J.H., Grave, W.S.D., Wolfhagen, I.H., & Vleuten, C.P.V.D. (2002). Trends in research on the tutor in problem-based learning: conclusions and implications for educational practice and research. *Medical Teacher, 24*(2), 173–180.

Driscoll, M.P. (2000). *Psychology for instruction*. London: Pearson.

Dunlosky, J., Rawson, K.A., Marsh, E.J., Nathan, M.J., & Willingham, D.T. (2013). Improving students' learning with effective learning techniques: promising directions from cognitive and educational psychology. *Psychological Science in the Public Interest, 14*(1), 4–58.

Dunning, D. (2005). *Self-insight: Roadblocks and detours on the path to knowing thyself*. New York, NY: Psychology Press.

Ebbinghaus, H. (1885). *Über das Gedächtnis. Untersuchungen zur experimentellen Psychologie*. Leipzig: Verlag von Duncker & Humblot.

Edmonds, R. (1979). Effective schools for the urban poor. *Educational Leadership, 37*, 15–27.

Ehrlinger, J., & Shain, E.A. (2014). How accuracy in students' self-perceptions relates to success in learning. In V.A. Benassi, C.E. Overson, C.M. Hakala (Eds), *Applying science of learning in education: Infusing psychological science into the curriculum*. Retrieved from the Society for the Teaching of Psychology website: http://teachpsych.org/ebooks/asle2014/index.php

Elmore, R. (1996). Getting to scale with good educational practice. *Harvard Educational Review, 66*(1), 1–27.

Ericsson, A., & Pool, R. (2016). *Peak: Secrets from the new science of expertise*. Boston, MA: Houghton Mifflin Harcourt.

Evans, J.H. (1981) *What have we learned from Follow Through?: Implications for future R & D programs*. Washington, DC: National Institute of Education. (ERIC Document Reproduction Service No. ED244737.)

Eysenck, & Keane, M.T. (1990). *Cognitive psychology: A student's handbook*. Hove: Erlbaum.

Fiorella, L., & Mayer, R.E. (2016). Effects of observing the instructor draw diagrams on learning from multimedia messages. *Journal of Educational Psychology, 108*(4), 528–546.

Flavell, J.H. (1979). Metacognition and cognitive monitoring: a new area of cognitive-developmental inquiry. *American Psychologist, 34*, 906–911.

Flavell, J.H. (1985). *Cognitive development* (2nd edn). Englewood Cliffs, NJ: Prentice Hall.

Foer, J. (2011). *Moonwalking with Einstein: The art and science of remembering everything*. London: Penguin.

Gates, A.I. (1917). Recitation as a factor in memorizing. *Archives of Psychology, 6*(40).

Geake, J. (2009). *The brain at school: Educational neuroscience in the classroom*. London: McGraw-Hill Education (UK).

Geary, D.C. (2007). Educating the evolved mind: reflections and refinements. *Educating the Evolved Mind: Conceptual Foundations for an Evolutionary Educational Psychology*, 177–203. Charlotte, NC.

Gehlbach, H., Brinkworth, M.E., King, A.M., Hsu, L.M., McIntyre, J., & Rogers, T. (2016). Creating birds of similar feathers: leveraging similarity to improve teacher–student relationships and academic achievement. *Journal of Educational Psychology, 108*(3), 342.

Gravemeijer, K.P.E., & Kirschner, P.A. (2007). Naar meer evidencebased onderwijs? *Pedagogische Studiën, 84*, 463–472.

Hambrick, D.Z., Oswald, F.L., Altmann, E.M., Meinz, E.J., Gobet, F., & Campitelli, G. (2014). Deliberate practice: is that all it takes to become an expert? *Intelligence, 45*, 34–45.

Hatfield, B.E., & Williford, A.P. (2017). Cortisol patterns for young children displaying disruptive behavior: links to a teacher–child, relationship-focused intervention. *Prevention Science: The Official Journal of the Society for Prevention Research, 18*(1), 40–49.

Hattie, J. (2003). *Teachers make a difference: What is the research evidence?* Auckland: The University of Auckland.

Hattie, J. (2009). *Visible learning: A synthesis of over 800 meta-analyses relating to achievement.* Abingdon: Routledge.

Hattie, J. (2012). *Visible learning for teachers: Maximizing impact on learning.* Abingdon: Routledge.

Hattie, J. (2015). The applicability of visible learning to higher education. *Scholarship of Teaching and Learning in Psychology, 1*(1), 79–91.

Hattie, J., & Jaeger, R. (1998). Assessment and classroom learning: a deductive approach. *Assessment in Education: Principles, Policy & Practice, 5*(1), 111–122.

Hattie, J., & Timperley, H. (2007). The power of feedback. *Review of Educational Research, 77*(1), 81–112.

Hattie, J., & Yates, G.C. (2013). *Visible learning and the science of how we learn.* Abingdon: Routledge.

Hattie, J., Biggs, J., & Purdie, N. (1996). Effects of learning skills interventions on student learning: a meta-analysis. *Review of Educational Research, 66*(2), 99–136.

Hayes, M.S., & Gershenson, S. (2016). What differences a day can make: quantile regression estimates of the distribution of daily learning gains. *Economics Letters, 141*, 48–51.

Hill, H.C., Charalambous, C.Y., & Kraft, M.A. (2012). When rater reliability is not enough: teacher observation systems and a case for the generalizability study. *Educational Researcher, 41*(2), 56–64.

Hooge, E.H., Janssen, S.K., Look, van K., Moolenaar, N., & Sleegers, P. (2015). *Bestuurlijk vermogen in het primair onderwijs. Mensen verbinden en inhoudelijk op een lijn krijgen om adequaat te sturen op onderwijskwaliteit.* Tilburg: TIAS School for Business and Society, Tilburg University.

Hsieh, I.L.G., & O'Neill, H.F. (2002). Types of feedback in a computer-based collaborative problem-solving group task. *Computers in Human Behavior, 18*, 699–715.

Jacob, R., & Parkinson, J. (2015). The potential for school-based interventions that target executive function to improve academic achievement: a review. *Review of Educational Research*, *85*(4), 512–552.

Jaehnig, W., & Miller, M.L. (2007). Feedback types in programmed instruction: a systematic review. *The Psychological Record*, *57*, 219–232.

Jamet, E., & Le Bohec, O. (2007). The effect of redundant text in multimedia instruction. *Contemporary Educational Psychology*, *32*(4), 588–598.

Johnson, Z.D., & LaBelle, S. (2017). An examination of teacher authenticity in the college classroom. *Communication Education*, *66*(4), 423–439.

Jones, S.M., Bailey, R., & Jacob, R. (2014). Social-emotional learning is essential to classroom management. *Phi Delta Kappan*, *96*(2), 19–24.

Jones, V.F., & Jones, L.S. (2012). *Comprehensive classroom management: Creating communities of support and solving problems* (10th edn). Upper Saddle River, NJ: Pearson.

Kalyuga, S. (2007). Expertise reversal effect and its implications for learner-tailored instruction. *Educational Psychology Review*, *19*(4), 509–539.

Kalyuga, S. (2014). The expertise reversal principle in multimedia learning. *The Cambridge handbook of multimedia learning*, 576–597. Cambridge: Cambridge University Press.

Kalyuga, S., Ayres, P., Chandler, P., & Sweller, J. (2003). The expertise reversal effect. *Educational Psychologist*, *38*(1), 23–31.

Kamphuis, E., & Vernooy, K. (2011). Feedback geven. Een sterke leerkracht-vaardigheid. *Basisschoolmanagement, jrg, 25*, 4–9.

Kang, S.H. (2016). Spaced repetition promotes efficient and effective learning: Policy implications for instruction. *Policy Insights from the Behavioral and Brain Sciences*, *3*(1), 12–19.

Karpicke, J.D., & Grimaldi, P.J. (2012). Retrieval-based learning: a perspective for enhancing meaningful learning. *Educational Psychology Review*, *24*, 401–418.

Kennedy, J. (1995). Debiasing the curse of knowledge in audit judgment. *Accounting Review*, 249–273.

Kerfoot, B.P., DeWolf, W.C., Masser, B.A., Church, P.A., & Federman, D.D. (2007). Spaced education improves the retention of clinical knowledge by medical students: a randomised controlled trial. *Medical Education*, *41*(1), 23–31.

Kidron, Y., & Lindsay, J. (2014). The effects of increased learning time on student academic and nonacademic outcomes: findings from a meta-analytic review. REL 2014-015. Regional Educational Laboratory Appalachia.

Kirschner, P.A., & van Merriënboer, J.J. (2013). Do learners really know best? Urban legends in education. *Educational Psychologist*, *48*(3), 169–183.

Kirschner, P.A., Sweller, J., & Clark, R.E. (2006). Why minimal guidance during instruction does not work: an analysis of the failure of constructivist, discovery, problem-based, experiential, and inquiry-based teaching. *Educational Psychologist, 41*(2), 75–86.

Korpershoek, H., Harms, T., de Boer, H., van Kuijk, M., & Doolaard, S. (2016). A meta-analysis of the effects of classroom management strategies and classroom management programs on students' academic, behavioral, emotional, and motivational outcomes. *Review of Educational Research, 86*(3), 643–680.

Kratochwill, T., DeRoos, R., & Blair, S. (2014). What works in classroom management. In R.E. Slavin (Ed.), *Proven programs in education: Classroom management and assessment*. Thousand Oaks, CA: Corwin Press.

Kurland, H., Peretz, H., & Hertz-Lazarowitz, R. (2010). Leadership style and organizational learning: the mediate effect of school vision. *Journal of Educational Administration, 48*(1), 7–30.

Lavery, L. (2008). *Self-regulated learning for academic success: An evaluation of instructional techniques* (Doctoral dissertation). Auckland: ResearchSpace.

Leary, T. (1957). *An interpersonal diagnosis of personality*. New York: The Ronald Press Company.

Leutwyler, B. (2009). Metacognitive learning strategies: differential development patterns in high school. *Metacognition and Learning, 4*, 111–123.

Levine, D., & Lezotte, L. (1990). *Unusually effective schools: A review of research and practice*. Madison, WI: National Center for Effective Schools Research and Development.

Lindsey, R.V., Shroyer, J.D., Pashler, H., & Mozer, M.C. (2014). Improving students' long-term knowledge retention through personalized review. *Psychological Science, 25*(3), 639–647.

Locke, E.A., & Latham, G.P. (2002). Building a practically useful theory of goal setting and task motivation: a 35-year odyssey. *American Psychologist, 57*, 705–717.

Logan, G.D. (1988). Toward an instance theory of automatization. *Psychological Review, 95*(4), 492.

Lommel, S., Laenen, A., & d'Ydewalle, G. (2006). Foreign-grammar acquisition while watching subtitled television programmes. *British Journal of Educational Psychology, 76*(2), 243–258.

Macnamara, B.N., Hambrick, D.Z., & Oswald, F.L. (2014). Deliberate practice and performance in music, games, sports, education, and professions: a meta-analysis. *Psychological Science, 25*, 1608–1618.

Macnamara, B.N., Moreau, D., & Hambrick, D.Z. (2016). The relationship between deliberate practice and performance in sports: a meta-analysis. *Perspectives on Psychological Science, 11*(3), 333–350.

Mainhard, M.T., Brekelmans, M., den Brok, P., & Wubbels, T. (2011). The development of the classroom social climate during the first months of the school year. *Contemporary Educational Psychology, 36*(3), 190–200.

Mani, A., Mullainathan, S., Shafir, E., & Zhao, J. (2013). Poverty impedes cognitive function. *Science, 341*(6149), 976-980.

Marreveld, M. (2014). Een Meester Neemt Afscheid. *Didactief.* retrieved from https://didactiefonline.nl/blog/redactie/een-meester-neemt-afscheid.

Martin, A.J. (2013). Goal setting and personal best (PB) goals. In J. Hattie & E.M. Anderman (Eds), *International guide to student achievement* (pp. 356–358). New York, NY: Routledge.

Marzano, R.J. (2003). *What works in schools: Translating research into action.* Alexandria, VA: Association for Supervision and curriculum Development.

Marzano, R.J. (2007). Leadership and school reform factors. In T. Townsend (Ed.), *International handbook of school effectiveness and improvement* (pp. 597–614). New York: Springer.

Marzano, R.J., & Pickering, D.J. (2007). Special topic: the case for and against homework. *Educational Leadership, 64*(6), 74–79.

Maslowski, R. (2006). A review of inventories for diagnosing school culture. *Journal of Educational Administration, 44*(1), 6–35.

Masschelein, J., & Simons, M. (2012). *Apologie van de school: Een publieke zaak* [In defense of the school: a public cause]. Leuven: Acco.

Mayer, R.E. (2009). *Multimedia learning* (2nd edn). New York: Cambridge University Press.

Mayer, R.E., & Anderson, R.B. (1992). The instructive animation: helping students build connections between words and pictures in multimedia learning. *Journal of Educational Psychology, 4,* 444–452.

Mayer, R.E., Lee, H., & Peebles, A. (2014). Multimedia learning in a second language: a cognitive load perspective. *Applied Cognitive Psychology, 28*(5), 653–660.

McGaghie, W.C., Issenberg, S.B., Cohen, M.E.R., Barsuk, J.H., & Wayne, D.B. (2011). Does simulation-based medical education with deliberate practice yield better results than traditional clinical education? A meta-analytic comparative review of the evidence. *Academic Medicine: Journal of the Association of American Medical Colleges, 86*(6), 706.

Muijs, D. (2016). *Leraareffectiviteit? Wat weten we (niet)?* ResearchED Amsterdam.

Muijs, D., Kyriakides, L., van der Werf, G., Creemers, B., Timperley, H., & Earl, L. (2014). State of the art – teacher effectiveness and professional learning. *School Effectiveness and School Improvement, 25*(2), 231–256.

Mullainathan, S., & Shafir, E. (2013). *Scarcity: Why having too little means so much.* Basingstoke: Macmillan.

Mullen, B., & Copper, C. (1994). The relation between group cohesiveness and performance: an integration. *Psychological Bulletin, 115*: 210–227.

Muller, D.A. (2008). *Designing effective multimedia for physics education* (Doctoral dissertation, University of Sydney, Australia).

Murre, J.M., & Dros, J. (2015). Replication and analysis of Ebbinghaus' forgetting curve. *PloS One*, *10*(7), e0120644.

Neves, D.M., & Anderson, J.R. (1981). Knowledge compilation: mechanisms for the automatization of cognitive skills. *Cognitive Skills and their Acquisition*, 57–84.

Obsuth, I., Murray, A.L., Malti, T., Sulger, P., Ribeaud, D., & Eisner, M. (2016). A non-bipartite propensity score analysis of the effects of teacher–student relationships on adolescent problem and prosocial behavior. *Journal of Youth and Adolescence*. DOI 10.1007/s10964-016-0534-y.

OECD (2016). *PISA 2015 Results (Volume II): Policies and Practices for Successful Schools*. Paris: OECD Publishing.

Oppenheimer, D.M. (2006). Consequences of erudite vernacular utilized irrespective of necessity: problems with using long words needlessly. *Applied Cognitive Psychology*, *20*(2), 139–156.

Paivio, A. (1971). Imagery and language. *Imagery: Current Cognitive Approaches*, 7–32. New York: Academic Press.

Palincsar, A.S. (1998). Keeping the metaphor of scaffolding fresh – a response to C. Addison Stone's 'The metaphor of scaffolding: Its utility for the field of learning disabilities'. *Journal of Learning Disabilities*, *31*(4), 370–373.

Pennebaker, J.W., & King, L.A. (1999). Linguistic styles: language use as an individual difference. *Journal of Personality and Social Psychology*, *77*(6), 1296.

Pinker, S. (2003). *The blank slate: The modern denial of human nature*. Penguin.

Porter, G.E., & Trifts, J.W. (2014). The career paths of mutual fund managers: the role of merit. *Financial Analysts Journal*, *70*(4), 55–71.

Reagh, Z.M., & Yassa, M.A. (2014). Repetition strengthens target recognition but impairs similar lure discrimination: evidence for trace competition. *Learning & Memory*, *21*(7), 342–346.

Remmers, H.H., & Remmers, E.M. (1926). The negative suggestion effect on true–false examination questions. *Journal of Educational Psychology*, *17*, 52–56.

Reynolds, D., Sammons, P., De Fraine, B., Van Damme, J., Townsend, T., Teddlie, C., & Stringfield, S. (2014). Educational effectiveness research (EER): a state-of-the-art review. *School Effectiveness and School Improvement*, *25*(2), 197–230.

Roediger, H.L., & Butler, A.C. (2011). The critical role of retrieval practice in long-term retention. *Trends in Cognitive Sciences*, *15*(1), 20–27.

Roediger III, H.L., & Karpicke, J.D. (2006). The power of testing memory: basic research and implications for educational practice. *Perspectives on Psychological Science*, *1*(3), 181–210.

Rohrer, D. (2012). Interleaving helps students distinguish among similar concepts. *Educational Psychology Review*, *24*, 355–367.

Rohrer, D., & Pashler, H. (2007). Increasing retention without increasing study time. *Current Directions in Psychological Science, 16*(4), 183–186.

Roorda, D.L., Koomen, H.M., Spilt, J.L., & Oort, F.J. (2011). The influence of affective teacher–student relationships on students' school engagement and achievement: a meta-analytic approach. *Review of Educational Research, 81*(4), 493–529.

Rosenshine, B. (2012). Principles of instruction: research-based strategies that all teachers should know. *American Educator, 36*(1), 12.

Rotter, J.B. (1967). A new scale for the measurement of interpersonal trust. *Journal of Personality, 35*(4), 651–665.

Sammons, P., Hillman, J., & Mortimore, P. (1995). *Key characteristics of effective schools: A review of school effectiveness research.* London: Ofsted.

Scheerens, J., (2013). What is effective schooling? A review of current thought and practice. International Baccalaureate Organization. Retrieved from www.ibo.org/globalassets/publications/ib-research/whatiseffectiveschoolingfinal-1.pdf.

Schneider, M., & Preckel, F. (2017). Variables associated with achievement in higher education: a systematic review of meta-analyses. *Psychological Bulletin, 143*(6), 565–600.

Schneider, W., Dumais, S.T., & Shiffrin, R.M. (1984). Automatic and control processing and attention. In R. Parasuraman & R. Davies (Eds), *Varieties of attention* (pp. 1–27). New York: Academic Press.

Schraw, G., Crippen, K.J., & Hartley, K. (2006). Promoting self-regulation in science education: metacognition as part of a broader perspective on learning. *Research in Science Education, 36*, 111–139.

Schuit, H., de Vrieze, I., & Sleegers, P. (2011). *Leerlingen motiveren: een onderzoek naar de rol van leraren* (Vol. 27). Ruud de Moor Centrum/ Open Universiteit.

Shakeshaft, N.G., Trzaskowski, M., McMillan, A., Rimfeld, K., Krapohl, E., Haworth, C.M., ... & Plomin, R. (2013). Strong genetic influence on a UK nationwide test of educational achievement at the end of compulsory education at age 16. *PLoS One, 8*(12), e80341.

Simons, P.R.J., & Verschaffel, L. (1992). Transfer: onderzoek en onderwijs. *Tijdschrift voor onderwijsresearch, 17*(1), 3–16.

Slavin, R.E. (2012). *Educational psychology: Theory and practice.* Upper Saddle River, NJ: Pearson.

Soderstrom, N.C., & Bjork, R.A. (2015). Learning versus performance: an integrative review. *Perspectives on Psychological Science, 10*(2), 176–199.

Sparrow, B., Liu, J., & Wegner, D.M. (2011). Google effects on memory: cognitive consequences of having information at our fingertips. *Science, 333*, 776–778.

Spilt, J.L., Koomen, H.M., & Thijs, J.T. (2011). Teacher wellbeing: the importance of teacher–student relationships. *Educational Psychology Review, 23*(4), 457–477.

Spitzer, H.F. (1939). Studies in retention. *Journal of Educational Psychology*, 30, 641–657.

Storm, B.C., & Stone, S.M. (2015). Saving-enhanced memory: the benefits of saving on the learning and remembering of new information. *Psychological Science, 26*(2), 182–188.

Sung, E., & Mayer, R.E. (2012). When graphics improve liking but not learning from online lessons. *Computers in Human Behavior, 28*(5), 1618–1625.

Sweller, J. (1988). Cognitive load during problem solving: effects on learning. *Cognitive Science, 12*(2), 257–285.

Sweller, J., Van Merriënboer, J.J., & Paas, F.G. (1998). Cognitive architecture and instructional design. *Educational Psychology Review, 10*(3), 251–296.

Timperley, H., Wilson, A., Barrar, H., & Fung, I. (2007). *Best evidence synthesis iterations (BES) on professional learning and development.* Wellington, NZ: Ministry of Education.

Tulving, E., & Arbuckle, T.Y. (1963). Sources of intratrial interference in immediate recall of paired associates. *Journal of Verbal Learning and Verbal Behavior, 1*(5), 321–334.

Turkheimer, E., Haley, A., Waldron, M., D'Onofrio, B., & Gottesman, I.I. (2003). Socioeconomic status modifies heritability of IQ in young children. *Psychological Science, 14*(6), 623–628.

Van der Kleij, F.M., Feskens, R.C., & Eggen, T.J. (2015). Effects of feedback in a computer-based learning environment on students' learning outcomes: a meta-analysis. *Review of Educational Research, 85*(4), 475–511.

Van Tartwijk, J., Mainhard, T., Brekelmans, M., Den Brok, P., & Levy, J. (2014). Docent-leerling interacties en het sociaal klimaat in de klas. In J. Van Tartwijk, M. Brekelmans, P. Den Brok & T. Mainhard (Eds), *Theorie en praktijk van leren en de leraar: Liber Amicorum Theo Wubbels* (pp. 25–43). Amsterdam: Uitgeverij SWP.

Veenman, M.V.J. (2013). Training metacognitive skills in students with availability and production deficiencies. In H. Bembenutty, T. Cleary, & A. Kitsantas (Eds), *Applications of self-regulated learning across diverse disciplines: A tribute to Barry J. Zimmerman* (pp. 299–324). Charlotte, NC: Information Age Publishing.

Veenman, M.V.J., & Spaans, M.A. (2005). Relation between intellectual and metacognitive skills: age and task differences. *Learning and Individual Differences, 15*, 159–176.

Veenman, M.V.J., Wilhelm, P., & Beishuizen, J.J. (2004). The relation between intellectual and metacognitive skills from a developmental perspective. *Learning and Instruction, 14*, 89–109.

Veenman, S. (2001). *Directe instructie. Paper ten behoeve van de cursus Instructievaardigheden*. Sectie Onderwijs en Educatie. Katholieke Universiteit Nijmegen.

Vergauwe, J., Wille, B., Feys, M., De Fruyt, F., & Anseel, F. (2015). Fear of being exposed: the trait-relatedness of the impostor phenomenon and its relevance in the work context. *Journal of Business and Psychology*, *30*(3), 565–581.

Vermunt, J.D.H.M. (1992). *Leerstijlen en sturen van leerprocessen in het hoger onderwijs. Naar procesgerichte instructie in zelfstandig denken.* Amsterdam: Swets & Zeitlinger.

Vermunt, J.D.H.M. (1998). Onderwijskundig Lexicon, Deel III. Leeractiviteiten van leerlingen. L. Verschaffel & J.D.H.M. Vermunt (Red.), *Het leren van leerlingen*, 29846. Alphen Aan De Rijn: Samson.

Vygotsky, L. (1978). Interaction between learning and development. *Readings on the development of children*, *23*(3), 79–91.

Walberg, H.J., & Tsai, S.L. (1983). Matthew effects in education. *American Educational Research Journal*, *20*(3), 359–373.

Wiliam, D. (2010). An integrative summary of the research literature and implications for a new theory of formative assessment. In H.L. Andrade & G.J. Cizek (Eds), *Handbook of formative assessment* (pp. 18–40). New York, NY: Taylor & Francis.

Wiliam, D. (2011). *Embedded formative assessment.* Bloomington, IN: Solution Tree Press.

Wiliam, D. (2012). Feedback: part of a system. *Educational Leadership*, *70*(1), 30–34.

Willingham, D.T. (2009). *Why don't students like school? A cognitive scientist answers questions about how the mind works and what it means for the classroom.* Hoboken, NJ: John Wiley & Sons.

Willingham, D.T. (2012). *When can you trust the experts?: How to tell good science from bad in education.* Hoboken, NJ: John Wiley & Sons.

Wood, D., Bruner, J.S., & Ross, G. (1976). The role of tutoring in problem solving. *Journal of Child Psychology and Psychiatry*, *17*(2), 89–100.

Woodbury, M.G., & Kuhnke, J.L. (2014). What's the difference? *Wound Care Canada*, *12*(1).

Wray, D. & Medwell, J. (2001). *What can teachers of literacy learn from a study of effective teachers?* Paper presented at the 12th European Reading Conference, Dublin, Ireland, 1–4 July. Retrieved from http://files.eric.ed.gov/fulltext/ED454500.pdf.

Wubbels, T. (2014). Leraar-leerlingrelaties in de klas: toekomst voor onderzoek. *Pedagogische Studiën*, (91) 352–363.

Wubbels, Th., Brekelmans, M. & Hooymayers H.P. (1993). Comparison of teachers' and students' perceptions of interpersonal teacher behavior. In T. Wubbels, & J. Levy (Eds). *Do you know what you look like?* (pp. 64–80). London: Falmer.

Wubbels, Th., Brekelmans, M., den Brok, P., & Tartwijk, J. van (2006). An interpersonal perspective on classroom management in secondary classrooms in the Netherlands. In C. Evertson, & C. Weinstein (Eds),

Handbook of classroom management: Research, practice, and contemporary issues (pp. 1161–1192). Mahwah, NJ: Lawrence Erlbaum.

Yassa, M.A., & Reagh, Z.M. (2013). Competitive trace theory: a role for the hippocampus in contextual interference during retrieval. *Frontiers in Behavioral Neuroscience, 7*, 107.

Yates, F. (1966). *The art of memory.* London: Routledge & Kegan Paul.

Yeager, D.S., Purdie-Vaughns, V., Hooper, S.Y., & Cohen, G.L. (2017). Loss of institutional trust among racial and ethnic minority adolescents: a consequence of procedural injustice and a cause of life-span outcomes. *Child Development, 88*(2), 658–676.

Yue, C.L., Bjork, E.L., & Bjork, R.A. (2013). Reducing verbal redundancy in multimedia learning: an undesired desirable difficulty? *Journal of Educational Psychology, 105*(2), 266.

Zimmerman, B.J. (2002). Becoming a self-regulated learner: an overview. *Theory into Practice, 41*(2), 64–70.

INDEX